Dr. Miles

The Life of
Dr. Franklin Lawrence Miles (1845-1929)

Martha M. Pickrell

TM

Guild Press of Indiana
Carmel, IN 46032

Library of Congress Number 97-77133

ISBN: 1-57860-023-5

CONTENTS

PREFACE

In 1984, the Miles, Inc. pharmaceutical company in Elkhart, Indiana (now known as Bayer) celebrated its 100th anniversary with a company history[1] and the development of professionally managed corporate archives. Leading this effort were Dr. Franz Geks, then CEO; Doloris Cogan, director of public relations; and Dr. Donald N. Yates, archivist. Among many other accomplishments, Dr. Yates did oral histories, interviewing company principals and descendants of the founder, Dr. Franklin Miles.

Having previously written about the career of Dr. Miles, I was asked to join the Miles Centennial project as a consultant, to gather additional information for the Miles Archives and for the the history's author, William Cray.

As my work ended, I was encouraged to consider using what had been gathered on Dr. Miles in some sort of biography; and two years after leaving the company's employ I wrote the first draft of this book. The text has evolved over a period of several years. What I have tried to do is to document his very full life with emphasis on his role as a physician and entrepreneur.

In my research, the staffs of many archives and libraries have been helpful. In the Elkhart area, aid has come from the Miles Archives, Elkhart Public Library, Ruthmere Museum, Elkhart County Historical Society, Elkhart County Recorder and Health Department, Elkhart County Medical Association, Mennonite Archives, Elkhart City Cemeteries, Tom Gutermuth, and Jack Linton.

In Chicago, I received help from the archives of the American Medical Association, Rush-Presbyterian-St. Luke's Medical School, and Northwestern University Medical School, and from the Chicago Historical Society and Chicago Public Library. In Fort Myers, Florida, help came from the Fort Myers Public Library, Fort Myers Historical Museum, Lee County offices, and Prudy Taylor Board.

Others have included the Ohio State Historical Society, the Cemetery of Spring Grove (Cincinnati), Allen County Public Library (Fort

Wayne, Indiana), Archives of the State of Hawaii; and the archives of the University of Michigan and Yale, Columbia, and Harvard Universities, Williston Academy, Northampton, Massachusetts, and Phillips Academy, Andover, Massachusetts.

Perhaps the most important sources of all have been the remembrances of family members, including Dr. Miles' daughter, Louise Miles Bass of Fort Myers, Florida, and three grandchildren, all now deceased: Elisabeth Miles Crow, Charles Foster Miles, and Franklin Beardsley Miles. A great-granddaughter, Susan Miles Yeckel, also has given a very important family perspective.

I wish to thank especially for their encouragement Mrs. Cogan; Dr. Yates; the Rev. George Minnix, formerly curator of Ruthmere Museum; Kathleen Gray, the present curator; and Dr. Patrick Furlong, history professor at Indiana University South Bend. Bob Pickrell, my late husband, gave unfailing and loving support.

"No man can be truly happy, without doing all in his power to contribute to the welfare of mankind."
—Franklin L. Miles, letter to his uncle
A. G. Lawrence, Feb. 22, 1867.

"The deed is the proof of faith, the test of character, and the standard of worth."
—Bishop Spalding, 1902; from an item passed down by Dr. Miles to his descendants.[1]

1
Introducing Dr. Miles

In the 1990s, amid the fast pace of everything around us, we are more and more encouraged to take charge of our own health. Our cost-conscious healthcare system is emphasizing preventive medicine—changes in lifestyle, diet, exercise, work, environment.

We are aware, too, of the importance of taking some control over the process of medical treatment. We read. We experiment. We try more than one physician. We try aspects of so-called "alternative medicine." And, as we have for a long, long time, we self-medicate, buying over-the-counter preparations which have been so perfected that many are as effective as prescription drugs.

Dr. Franklin Lawrence Miles, more than a century ago, already saw these needs and provided solutions. His nonprescription remedies were designed to lessen stress and promote better regulation of the body's normal functions. And he was truly a pioneer in popular health education. His medical pamphlets reached millions of homes with specific advice on all aspects of healthy daily living. He admonished physicians, too, to pay as much attention to maintaining health as to treating disease. In many ways, he was a man far ahead of his time.

A major figure in bringing medicinal relief to the great mass of the American people from the 1880s to the 1920s, Miles was a hard-working medical practitioner who prepared his first bottles of nerve tranquilizer on a stove in his home in the small city of Elkhart, Indiana.

His unique character can be glimpsed from a number of angles. A first image comes from remembrances of Bill Rich of Elkhart. "He was thinking all the time. He walked all over the sidewalk. He could pass you on the street without seeing you."[1] Miles had an ever-inquiring, creative, entrepreneurial mind. To question, to investigate, to remedy or solve, to invent and promote—these purposes drove him throughout his life.

A second image comes from engravings in his early advertising: a pale, severe, scholarly face, with prematurely bald forehead, flowing beard, set mouth, and stern eyes keenly focused behind round Victorian spectacles. Gradually replaced by older versions of the same serious visage, this "institutional" Dr. Miles addressed the public from countless flyers and pamphlets.

On one level, this image was highly effective in advertising; yet it was a true image, with a deep basis in his character. Miles was a deeply guarded person and very sensitive to injustice, beginning with a youth full of sorrows and struggles. He assiduously cultivated his physical strength, and was well versed in the law.

He would need this toughness because, like other physician-entrepreneurs of his time, he came to occupy an uncomfortable position. By developing proprietary remedies he forfeited the official approval of the medical community and was inevitably labeled by them a patent-medicine "quack."

He used his toughness in devising defensive strategies, not only in his medical career but also in other business dealings. On a wider stage, he attacked with his pen the world's injustices, from the shocking infant mortality rate in the United States to the oppression of Cubans by Spain. And he was so dissatisfied with the general state of America's health and health care that he continually worked to make some improvement.

A third image looks out at us from family photographs: a tanned, vigorous-looking gentleman of seventy-five, flawlessly dressed in a tropical-weight business suit, sporting a toupee, holding a cigar, standing under the palm trees of his Florida estate with his family of children and grandchildren, some of whom tower over his short, stocky figure.[2]

This was the congenial private man Miles became, at ease in his large inner circle of family, friends, neighbors, and employees. This was the loving, strict, very concerned father and grandfather described with affection in the reminiscences of his grandchildren and of Louise Miles Bass, the daughter he and his second wife Elizabeth adopted when he was in his sixties.

This was the teacher of strong moral values to the younger generations. This was the "boss" known for his quiet authority and wise fairness. And this was the accessible, modest, unpretentious fellow who enjoyed a fishing outing, a game of poker, and a good story or prank.

A final key to Miles may be found in a book. He was fond of the popular eighteenth-century guide to manners and morals, Lord Chesterfield's *Letters to His Son.*[3] To succeed with people, Chesterfield wrote, a gentleman must display gracious manners, perfect speech and dress, and a bearing of unruffled calm and dignity. Underneath, he must be as firm as a rock, revealing his innermost thoughts only to the most trustworthy friend, never yielding on a point of importance. In his work habits, a gentleman must be active, methodical, and thorough, concentrating on each subject until it was completely mastered.

Like Chesterfield, Miles, too, with all his restless creativity, developed a rational, self-disciplined, prudent, broad-minded approach to the world. It was a realistic view, one in which troubles and human foibles were to be expected, most learning did not come from books, and various customs and religions deserved respect.

2
Early Life and Education, 1845-1875

A Difficult Youth

Franklin Lawrence Miles was born about 1845[1] at Olmsted Falls, near Cleveland, Ohio, into a difficult world, one very different from our own. For the people who lived in the settlements near the lakes and rivers of the new West—even people who were relatively prosperous—good health and long life were not the norm. Causes of most diseases were unknown, and medicine, with its crude techniques of bloodletting and purgation, applied to all patients alike, was almost helpless.

The hardships of western living made matters worse: malaria-producing swamps, an unbalanced diet, poor sanitation, poor building construction and heating, difficult travel. Economic uncertainty, too, afflicted the majority of people, even including Franklin's father and mother, Charles Julius and Electa Lawrence Miles, who came from proud, relatively affluent families.

Charles Julius Miles' maternal grandfather, Major Lorenzo Carter, was a founder of the city of Cleveland, and his mother, Laura Carter, its first white native. Erastus Miles, Charles' father, was a leading Cleveland businessman. The Lawrences of Massachusetts proudly pointed to their descent from the Dukes of Normandy. Electa Lawrence Miles' brother-in-law, Edward Stow Hamlin, was a prominent Ohio lawyer and served in Congress.[2]

As a young man, Charles Julius Miles tried numerous business efforts, and served one session as a clerk in the Ohio legislature. Somewhat later, as a man with a young family, he did what so many others did in the Gold Rush era: set out on his own for the far West. During Franklin's childhood his father found his way, not just to California, but eventually to the Sandwich Islands (Hawaii), where he served as Custom House Surveyor and Guard at the Port of Honolulu.

Franklin was one of three children. For some years Electa Miles, left in Ohio, coped with the raising of young Franklin, his younger sister Kate and little brother Charles. Keeping close to Edward Stow Hamlin, a widower with a family of his own, Electa Miles and her family moved to Columbus, then to Elyria, and finally to Cincinnati on the broad Ohio.[3]

We have few records of Franklin's own childhood, but from later evidence it appears that fishing and other outdoor activities brought him happiness. He had a healthy sense of "scientific curiosity," too, according to a quote from one of his later publications: "When a small boy he began his career by dissecting cats, frogs, fish, and in fact anything that he could lay his hands on."[4]

Emotionally, however, there was great difficulty. In later writings, Franklin Miles would lament the absence of his father during his childhood.[5] And at the age of about eleven he experienced one of the worst catastrophes that can happen to a child. Suddenly, in a period of seven months, death robbed him of his mother, brother and sister.

Cincinnati cemetery records tell the grim story. First came the death of his four-year-old brother Charles, of pneumonia, in May, 1856; then of nine-year-old Kate, of smallpox, in December, 1856. Finally, Electa Miles, who had been suffering from consumption, died in January, 1857.[6] In her dying days, she told Franklin that she wanted him to study the sciences—a wish that would have great impact on his life.[7]

With his father still in Hawaii, Franklin became, in effect, an orphan. A boy who found himself alone in life needed to cultivate adult qualities of self-sufficiency, needed to deal privately with his thoughts and fears. A few years later, he would refer to himself as having become "extremely suspicious" and "unsocial" as a result of being deprived of his parents.[8]

One source of suspicion, he later told his daughter, was that the aunt and uncle with whom he went to live were poor substitute parents. The uncle, at least, treated him shabbily. Franklin finally confronted him, and, with the aid of his more sympathetic aunt, secured better treatment.[9]

Franklin's father did keep in communication. He wrote Franklin fascinating letters describing his travels and detailing the customs of the Hawaiians, whom he much admired. Franklin must have taken hope when his father returned to America late in 1860, bringing collections of Hawaiian artifacts and shells.[10]

Charles Julius Miles decided to settle in Elkhart, Indiana, a small but thriving town on the St. Joseph and Elkhart rivers surrounded by rich agricultural country. Founded in 1832 by Dr. Havilah Beardsley, Elkhart had 1,500 people by 1860.

Charles had known Elkhart from his young manhood. In 1837 he had tried his luck as a merchant in partnership with Samuel Strong, a nephew of his mother's second husband, James Strong of Cleveland. By 1860, Samuel Strong had become one of Elkhart's leading merchants. Charles' mother, Laura Carter Miles Strong, also lived in Elkhart, perhaps coming at the same time as her son. Charles became a storekeeper on North Main Street.[11]

Franklin, now in his teens, lived with his father (or possibly with the Samuel Strongs) for about two or three years. Helping his father in the store, possibly attending school, in his free hours he enjoyed boating on the river with boy companions. A few years later, Franklin wrote, "I have no taste for business, my experience at Elkhart proved that plainly."[12] No doubt Franklin Miles sensed that he needed a freer, more venturesome, more challenging life.

Letters from Charles to his son, in fact, indicate that at some point Franklin went to live with his uncle A. G. Lawrence in Adrian, Michigan. By May, 1864, he was helping his uncle Edward Stow Hamlin on what was called "the old farm," Hamlin's summer home in western Massachusetts. And that fall, Franklin enrolled at Williston Seminary in nearby Northampton.[13]

In his letters, though he did not write often, Charles Miles seemed to regret his son's leaving. He admonished him to live virtuously and unextravagantly, and repeatedly praised a new boy assistant at the store, who was "steady as a deacon." He revealed that in Elkhart Franklin had had some sort of experiences with ghosts or spirits, "especially that part when you left the back door of (the) store open." He urged his son to progress "rapidly *(in your studies)* as possible considering your eyes."[14]

Problems with his health and enjoyment of outdoor life may have been just two of a number of factors prolonging Franklin Miles' education. He had difficulties not just with his eyes, but also with his digestive system. He had a certain lack of purpose and studiousness, and there was a self-confessed "wildness" of behavior.[15] Miles was at least eighteen years old when he entered Williston, a boys' preparatory school which was Congregational in origin. He was a second-year student.

Williston's strict, tireless headmaster, Marshall Henshaw, emphasized science instruction. Miles was virtually the only midwestern student in the English Department, which was designed "to occupy an intermediate place between the ordinary Academy or High School, and the scientific departments of College."

For middle-year students, the course of study included algebra and geometry, anatomy and physiology, and bookkeeping. A large new gymnasium was open "for the constant use of the students out of school hours" as well as required gymnastics.[16]

Miles' autograph book, full of comments from new friends, indicates that his life at Williston was far from over-studious, and that he had found relief from his customarily "unsocial" life. A classmate wrote, "Although regretting that your career at Williston Seminary has not been unblemished, or your name unspotted in the far-seeing eyes of 'Ye Professors,' yet, dear youth, I am much consoled by noticing your high standing in the hearts of your school-mates . . . ."[17]

Staying at Williston till the spring of 1865, and likely revisiting his uncle's farm that summer, he then transferred to Phillips Academy at Andover, Massachusetts. This proud old institution was directed by Samuel Harvey Taylor, a classicist and a strong character who drove his pupils by sheer will power. Rather than emphasizing the classics, however, Miles was enrolled, again, in the "English Department."

He studied until 1866 at Andover, but did not graduate; there is a family story that he was "canned" for some prank. His autograph book and letters indicate that he may have made some close friends in Andover, including at least one young woman.[18]

High school graduation was not required for college entrance at that time. After another summer on the Hamlin farm, Miles enrolled in the fall of 1866 as a special student at the Sheffield Scientific School at Yale. And thus began a collegiate career that would extend until 1875, encompassing the worlds of science, law, and medicine. For various reasons, he would give almost equal attention to the development of physical skills and sports such as gymnastics, running, riflery, horsemanship, and boxing.[19]

He was now completely alone, for his father had died shortly after he entered Andover, and his grandmother the year before. To support his studies and living expenses, he received funds from his father's estate (paid to him periodically by Samuel Strong), and also from his uncle A. G. Lawrence.

Miles kept his connection with Elkhart, and returned periodically to the city. In later years, Miles told his daughter that he had used much of his inheritance foolishly, and finally finished his education with the aid of such jobs as tutoring, stoking furnaces, and waiting tables.[20]

A Budding Scientist/Entrepreneur

Miles' carefully preserved letters, essays and notes provide intimate glimpses of his life from early 1867 until perhaps a year or more before his entrance into medical school in 1871. They reveal a young man searching for a vocation amid advice from his relatives, gradually becoming a self-motivated student and would-be entrepreneur, and focusing his attention especially on the new sciences related to breeding and genetics.

They show a young man looking for role models in great men of the past, and influenced by intellectual trends of his time such as Darwinism, spiritualism, phrenology, and women's rights, and by popular philosophers like P. T. Barnum. They show a young man decidedly questioning in matters of religion, and forming broad concepts of humanitarian service.

They also reveal a young man with physical and emotional problems, lonely and much missing a family life, and struggling with thoughts about his own moral nature. They reveal a young bachelor naturally preoccupied with winning women's confidence. Lighter moods are revealed in a number of the letters.

Miles chose Yale's Sheffield Scientific School with his mother's last request in mind. Founded in 1847 by chemist Benjamin Silliman and others, Sheffield offered instruction in science, mathematics, agriculture, and engineering to undergraduate, graduate, and special students.

The school had its own three-story building containing lecture rooms, laboratories, library, and specimen collections. Sheffield students went on collecting excursions as well to add specimens to the new Peabody Museum. Each student worked closely with a specific instructor. Specialization was encouraged.

Sheffield also was a place of enjoyment. Its students led a comparatively privileged existence. They had "no dormitories, no required chapel, no disciplinary marks, and no proctor." They did participate in Yale's literary societies and sports, and like other Yale students, relaxed after supper on the college fence, smoking and chatting.[21]

According to his letters of January to March, 1867, however, Miles' life in New Haven was not particularly happy. His lodgings were not as pleasant as those at Andover. He had a chronic case of "dyspepsia," which was so severe that he could barely concentrate on his studies. He battled it with a spare diet of bread, water, potatoes, vegetables, and a little meat, excluding all dairy products and rich foods, and with hours of exercise every day, four hours in the gymnasium plus daily runs of five miles or longer.

That winter, none of his studies appealed to him very much. He wrote Edward Stow Hamlin that if it were not for his mother's wishes, he might not be studying the sciences at all. Chemistry, for example, had not enthralled him. There was one very important exception, however. It was ichthyology, the study of fish. He wanted to pursue it seriously, in order to learn to breed fish as a business.

Sheffield had no books on "pisciculture," so he sent to New York for them. His uncle A. G. Lawrence was opposed to the idea, but Hamlin was enthusiastic, offering to go into business with him on the "old farm." To better prepare himself, Miles planned to enroll in the Laboratory of Natural History at Sheffield in the fall of 1867. He even contemplated studying with the great naturalist Jean Louis Agassiz of Harvard. Another subject favored by Miles was rhetoric, or argumentation.[22]

He was much concerned with standing higher in his uncles' eyes, and yet declaring his independence, his manhood. He responded to Lawrence's concern over his religion and future moral welfare with this: "I have reason, I hope, for thinking that my morals are not entirely corrupt. Perhaps I may have been wild...I think that I have gradually been attaining a strength, depth and firmness of character that I have not always possessed."

On religion, he wrote, "Though I am not and probably never will be a member of (a) church, yet I have...a kind of religion of my own," founded, he added, on what he considered a principle of self-interest: "No man can be truly happy, without doing all in his power to contribute to the welfare of mankind."[23]

About a year and a half later, in the late summer of 1868, Miles was still in New Haven, apparently well into his studies of zoology at Sheffield, and still searching for a likely spot for his fish farm.[24]

A letter written in early 1869 reveals some of his other interests. The four corners of his room were full of stacks of articles; finding his correspondent's letter would be like "searching a dung hill for a jewel." He was reading Confucius, and Abercrombie's *Intellectual Powers*. He had written brief sketches of 250 "great luminaries of the past...classified in order of birth." He put a few sample sketches into his letter book: Jonathan Swift, Lord Chesterfield, Edmund Burke.

A catalog of his library included thought-provoking works such as Darwin's *Origin of Species,* Emerson's *Society and Solitude* and Thoreau's *Letters,* lives of the presidents and of Socrates, and many others.[25]

Also in his library was a two-volume *History of the Supernatural.* He described the then-popular study of spiritualism in a letter to a woman friend as "our new religion in its various phases, religious and scientific..." He wrote, "You can't imagine how earnestly I feel inclined to work in behalf of this holy cause...so interesting, so inviting."[26]

In these years Miles joined the First Spiritualistic Association of New Haven. He was not uncritical of spiritualistic practices; in an essay he characterized nearly all mediums as fakes who were tolerated by serious spiritualists because they brought "more publicity for spiritualism." He ardently believed that spiritualism need not rely on such practitioners.[27]

Miles also took part in some of New Haven's scholarly debates. In one debate on women's rights, he took the negative side, writing a friend that women "are not sufficiently advanced in the secrets of political economy and government" to vote.[28]

In his letters of 1868-69, there are more glimpses of the dark side of his life, his loneliness and bouts of depression and continuing physical suffering from "dyspepsia." He still likely had trouble with his eyes; a friend writing in his autograph book in 1869 inquired, "How are your blinkers?"

In one letter, Miles wrote of spending Christmas alone, trying not to envy the happiness of others. In another letter, seeking a closer relationship with a woman, he wrote, "It is seldom that my unsocial nature permits me to form a friendship, but once formed, it is like unto a house built upon a rock, immoveable."[29]

At least one close relationship, that with his uncle Edward Stow Hamlin, was apparently damaged. In his letter to Samuel Strong in August 1868, Miles wrote bitterly that Hamlin had become cold toward him and no longer welcomed him at the farm. Miles expressed the belief that it was because he had turned down his uncle's offer of partnership in the fish business; but Hamlin's reported reason was hearing from Elkhart relatives of his nephew's reputation for less than "proper" behavior.[30]

Despite his earlier efforts to win their trust, his relatives, Miles feared, had decided he was "a man of no moral character or reliability." He admitted to sexual "wildness," to seeking "most any mode of excitement" to find "true sympathizing friends" and "dround *[sic]* the dull distressing thoughts" of his "socially isolated condition." To a woman friend, he referred to a "single imperfection of character" and "inaccuracies of deportment."[31]

Wrestling with thoughts about his moral character, he wrote "Austin" in April, 1969, "O! That I were an Adonis! but thank Heaven that I am not a Tarquin or even an Iago . . .. I have never robbed a man of his name, of his purse, nor anything that was my neighbor's except perhaps 'what he would lose again.' Experience is an indefatigable writer . . . . He has long been my only instructor, death having deprived me of all others; and many a moral lesson has he taught this pupil."[32]

In the same letter he showed some restlessness. He wrote, "I glory in the name of a cosmopolitan." He wanted to "shake the dust off my feet" and leave "this land of orthodoxy and loose virtue . . ." As the dream of the fish farm began to fade, Miles changed his focus of study to the world of human beings.[33]

In the fall of 1869, Miles enrolled in the Yale Law School. The school then had just a handful of students and a small library.[34] Little is known about his legal studies at Yale except that somewhere around this time he wrote in his letter book an essay on the Connecticut divorce law, agreeing with its liberality and arguing against the idea of marriage as a sacrament only the church could dissolve.

"What won't people do in the name of religion?" he argued. "They have shed the hearts blood of hundreds of thousands of their innocent brethren; burned men, women and children at the stake; forbid marriage altogether as the Quakers *[sic]* practiced polygamy as the ancient Jews...or the modern Mormons..." His concern for women's rights had advanced to the degree of believing in their right to leave an unsuitable marriage.[35]

In the fall of 1870, he moved to New York to intensify his legal studies. Columbia Law School was famed for its rigorous method of instruction instituted by Theodore William Dwight. Grueling daily written and oral examinations were supplemented by lectures on law and political science, and weekly moot courts.

Miles later claimed the title of LL.B., though he obtained no degree, because of having survived this course.[36] According to his own notes, he may also have studied at a "University of Phy. & Law" in New York.[37]

Though now well versed in the law, Miles still had not settled on a vocation. He later told his daughter that he believed he would be ineffectual in arguing cases in court because of his short stature.[38]

The world of science still beckoned. Notes in his letter book show that "scientific propagation of the human race" (an idea much discussed at the time) seemed the worthiest study of all. In his essay on divorce in Connecticut, he stated his concern that bad marriages would result in "bad children" and "lawless citizens." And he published an article in the *Phrenological Journal* in which he expressed admiration for the Greeks for their interbreeding of populations.[39] He may possibly now have fulfilled his dream of studying "embryology" with Prof. Agassiz at Harvard College.[40]

Going into business also was much on his mind, as shown by a list he made of "Modes of Making Money." "Practice Law" was one of eighteen suggestions. More fanciful ideas, showing familiarity with P. T. Barnum, included "Breed Monsters, as Barnum's Mermaid"; breed frogs or turtles for sale in Europe; create "Educational Games, viz., Geology, Biology, Philology, Chronology, Biography, etc."; make "waterproof wooden bottles" or "umbrellas with skylights" or a "steam frying pan" or "honey and maple sugar candies (advertise anti-poison)"; or "write a book upon Men who have traveled a short route to Fortune."

One important suggestion described a grand scheme: "1st. Write a book on the Scientific mode of Propagating the Human Race. 2nd. Lecture upon the Above Topic. 3rd. Start an Office, and give advice on the same."[41]

In further notes on his proposed "Propagation Business," he envisioned giving "advice by mail . . . have circulars, with questions relating to temperament of both parents and applicant, also hereditary diseases etc. and thus by the aid of this advice as to what kind of person should be the future wife or husband can be quite accurately given . . . . He would have "eminent men" fill out statistical forms: "This would be a mode of advertising as well as obtaining knowledge."[42]

He showed keen awareness of the new "science" of advertising. In notes on "Advertising," he wrote, "get written statements for all the noted men under whom I study, and I may use them when desirable...employ engravings, viz., those of eminent men, monsters, myself, etc...Employ apt quotations from eminent authors...Prof. Miles! Why was Tirah Colbin the greatest mental mathematician at the age of 6 and 10 years the world has ever produced, when his ancestors were remarkable for no mental trate *[sic]*—Read Prof. Miles' book and see."[43]

He copied quotes on the value of advertising as a route to success, including P. T. Barnum's: "Don't be above your business...select the right location; avoid debt; persevere; whatever you do, do with all your might; use the best tools; don't scatter your powers; be systematic; read the papers, beware of 'outside' operations; advertise your business; don't tell what you are going to do; have a good article;—advertising is the royal road to business."[44]

The Pursuit of Medicine

There is nothing definitive in Miles' letter book predicting his decision to study medicine. But very likely his interest in "scientific propagation" led him in this direction. Miles later told his daughter that a roommate who planned to be a doctor was a strong influence. And perhaps he now saw somewhat more clearly a useful way "to contribute to the welfare of mankind."[45] In the academic year 1871-72 he went to Ann Arbor, Michigan and enrolled in the University of Michigan's medical school, one of the nation's largest and best.[46]

Much progress was being made in medicine in the period during and after the Civil War. Yet medical education was still many years away from the great reforms ushered in by the founding of Johns Hopkins in 1889. The typical student at one of the handful of respectable medical colleges (there were many more shoddy ones) studied and apprenticed for three years with a competent physician and attended two sessions of lectures, usually of a few months each, ending in an examination and diploma.

Medical schools had no entrance requirements and attracted few college graduates. Clinical training was almost nonexistent. Instructional equipment was poor. The "basics" of anatomy, physiology, pathology and therapeutics were inadequately taught.[47]

But here and there, advances were being made; and Miles, in his years of medical study, plainly took advantage of them. The University of Michigan offered unusually good clinical instruction (though not true clinical experience) through its hospital and laboratory. Dr. Alonzo Benjamin Palmer, a leader in improving Michigan's instruction, taught Miles in "a private course of instruction in Diseases of the Heart and Lungs" and "The Art of Physical Diagnosis."[48]

The techniques of what later became known as internal medicine were then in their infancy. "Physical diagnosis" involved the use of diagnostic instruments and touching the patient. A pioneer of physical diagnosis was Dr. Austin Flint, whose classic *Practice of Medicine* (1868) was one of Miles' much-used textbooks.[49]

According to school records, Miles' preceptor in Elkhart, with whom he studied between sessions of medical school, was Dr. Oscar B. Harrington. Harrington was an 1862 Michigan graduate who had come to Elkhart from St. Joseph, Michigan, in 1869. His business card in the Elkhart newspapers described him as a physician and surgeon who paid "special attention to diseases of the throat and chest."[50]

Newspaper accounts show that Miles pursued other activities in Elkhart, such as taking the part of "Farmer Morton" in an amateur performance of "The Union Spy," and contributing articles to a local paper. One on "Stirpiculture" praised the Greeks for the wisdom of their "breeding" practices but denied their possibility in modern society. Another discussed fakery in spiritualism.[51]

In Elkhart, too, most importantly, Miles courted an Elkhart girl,

Ellen Lighthall, five years his junior. On April 22, 1873, they were married at St. John's Episcopal Church.[52]

No doubt an excellent remedy for Miles' self-labeled "suspicious," "unsocial" nature, Ellen Lighthall Miles was described as pretty, very musical, high-spirited, and popular with schoolmates. The daughter of Nathan Lighthall, a machinist and pioneer settler of the nearby city of Mishawaka, Ellen had taught school, had been active in St. John's— and now joined Franklin in medical studies. In the early fall of 1873 they went to Chicago, he to study at Rush Medical College, she to pursue the possibilities of obstetrics and gynecology.[53]

Their most unusual way of getting to Chicago was described in the *Elkhart Observer*. Miles fitted out a small boat, which they named the "Dot," to go down the St. Joseph River from Elkhart to St. Joseph, Michigan, where they would catch the steamer for Chicago. Edward and Emma Molloy, editors of the *Observer*, accompanied them part way, and Emma Molloy detailed their encounters with rainstorms, thirsty mosquitoes, and curious townspeople.

During the the course of the eighteen-day trip, Miles showed his mastery of the practical arts of hunting, fishing and tent camping. No doubt they undertook this trip, which offered considerable risk in the malarial season, in the spirit of an experiment as well as an excursion.[54]

Rush Medical College was functioning in makeshift quarters since the Great Chicago Fire of 1871 had leveled its buildings. Its frame building stood below the level of the raised street, and was known as "the college under the sidewalk." The school was near Cook County Hospital.

Despite its physical limitations, Rush offered excellent teaching and opportunities for clinical observation. Clinical instruction during at least one college term was required for graduation. The nearby hospital and charity clinics offered "the greatest variety of diseases and accidents" in such fields as gynecology, surgery, and the eye and ear.

Among prominent teachers at Rush were Dr. E. Fletcher Ingals, a well-known otolaryngologist, and Dr. Joseph Priestly Ross, professor of clinical medicine and diseases of the chest. In his later publications, Miles printed a letter of certification from Dr. Ross, certifying that Miles had "taken two of my courses of private instruction in Diseases of the Heart and Lungs, in the wards of Cook County Hospital."[55]

Other lectures he attended included Chemistry, Physiology, Principles and Practice of Medicine, General Therapeutics and Medical Jurisprudence, Surgical Anatomy and Military Surgery, and Diseases of the Brain and Nervous System.[56]

Miles received his M. D. degree from Rush Medical College on February 17, 1874. The graduates heard Dr. DeLaskie Miller, professor of obstetrics, expound at length on the unity of natural forces and elements in a Divine Will, the defects of the new evolutionary theory, the exalted nature of mankind, the vanity of medical "sects," and the nobility of medical science.[57]

The new M.D. opened an office in his residence at 57 Blue Island Avenue.[58] But he also continued his studies, apparently driven both by his interest in research and by the desire to acquire a "specialty."

Though few physicians could yet make a living through specializing, and almost invariably needed to rely on general practice as well, certain specialties were taking shape, and, in urban areas, starting to prove lucrative. The traditional doctor who practiced in patients' homes was beginning to be replaced by the doctor in his office, surrounded by specialized and expensive equipment.[59]

Miles chose to pursue a special interest in the nervous system. At lectures at Chicago Medical College (later Northwestern University Medical School), he came into contact with the new American school of neurology. One of its leading figures, Dr. J. S. Jewell, founder of the *Journal of Nervous and Mental Diseases*, was on the college faculty.[60]

No doubt Miles also became well acquainted with the umbrella-like concept of "neurasthenia," or functional nervous affliction, first developed by Dr. George A. Beard, a New York physician, in a number of articles and books. Beard wrote that "impoverishment of nerve force," caused by strain on the nervous system, brought about a host of symptoms, from exhaustion and lack of appetite, to irregular heartbeat, to severe mental problems.

Unlike many cases of disease, most neurasthenics could be successfully treated with combinations of rest, proper diet, and medication. The popularity of this "umbrella diagnosis" spread rapidly and helped fill physicians' calendars.[61]

The eye and ear especially drew Miles' interest, as most important organs of the nervous system. According to later writings, he completed two lecture courses at the Illinois Charitable Eye and Ear Infirmary, directed by Dr. Edward Holmes, a prominent member of the Rush faculty.

The Infirmary treated over 1,000 patients in 1873-74. Students could observe a wide variety of surgical procedures. In February, 1875, according to a letter Miles published from Holmes, Miles passed a special examination in diagnosis and treatment of eye and ear diseases.[62]

The impact of eye problems on the nervous system was an area that was beginning to receive needed attention. In his later writings, Miles showed familiarity with the studies of Dr. S. Weir Mitchell of Philadelphia, another of the foremost pioneers of American neurology, head of the nation's first clinic for nervous diseases and originator of a famous "rest cure" for neurasthenia.

Mitchell's articles of 1874 and 1875 broke new ground in linking certain cases of chronic and severe headache to eye strain and uncorrected visual defects. Eyeglasses were prescribed as a cure.[63]

As Dr. Miles completed his studies, Ellen Miles had continued her own. For awhile in 1874-75, Franklin and Ellen broke up housekeeping while Ellen lived at the Women's Hospital Medical College, a Chicago hospital for women and children, as "assistant physician and student." She completed a course in February, 1875. Earlier, she had attended Hahnemann Medical College, which was devoted to the then-popular study of homeopathy. Both husband and wife were now trained for the life of medicine.[64]

3
Growth of a Physician, 1875-1881

I n May, 1875, Franklin and Ellen Miles returned to Elkhart. They set up both their home and an office for Franklin in "one of the coziest little cottages" in town, at 7 Franklin Street, near the center of downtown. Miles announced in the newspapers that he would treat diseases of the eye and ear.[1] Ellen was pregnant with their first child.

Perhaps they may have considered staying in Chicago, with its greater prestige for an ambitious young doctor. But both Franklin and Ellen had family and friends in and around Elkhart. And the prospect of a successful medical practice in Elkhart no doubt seemed bright. There were just a handful of physicians to serve several thousand people in Elkhart, nearby Goshen (the county seat), and surrounding towns and rural area. There were no others who made a specialty of treating the eye and ear.

Elkhart's growth held promise. Like so many other American towns, it had rapidly industrialized since the Civil War. Paper mills and other factories had sprung up with the development of water power along the St. Joseph and Elkhart rivers. Hundreds of railroad employees had come to work in the new Lake Shore & Michigan Southern repair shops at the south end of town.

The flamboyant musician Charles G. Conn was just starting to manufacture mouthpieces for cornets, and the Rev. John Fretz Funk, head of the Mennonite Publishing Co., was establishing Elkhart as a center of printing and publishing. Women were going to work in factories, and in civic reform.

Doubling its population from 3,265 in 1870 to 6,939 in 1880, Elkhart advanced from town to city government status in the spring of 1875. Despite a pronounced building boom on Main Street, sidewalks, paved streets, sewers and water works were still in the future.[2]

Miles rapidly became prominent in the medical, social and intellectual life of the city. About a month after his arrival, the *Observer* reported that he had been elected secretary of the Elkhart Medical Society and had given a paper on "The Nervous System." A few days later, he was elected treasurer of the Elkhart County Medical Society.

Like Miles, most of his Elkhart colleagues were graduates of "regular" medical schools. They included Drs. Harrington, C. S. Frink, F. C. Eckelman, J. A. Work, R. Q. Haggerty, and others. Homeopathic and other "irregular" physicians also practiced in Elkhart County; the early medical societies to which Miles belonged purposely excluded them. These included a new Elkhart City Medical Society begun in June, 1877, by Miles, Eckelman, Frink, and others.[3]

With the aid of his attractive wife, Miles socialized with his fellow physicians. In the summer of 1875 he and Ellen Miles hosted the first meeting of an "Elkhart Medico-Socio-Society," designed to fill in the months when meetings of the medical societies were suspended.[4]

In addition to their Elkhart friends, the Miles enjoyed a family circle that included Nathan and Sarah Lighthall—Ellen's father and stepmother—and the Samuel Strongs. Most importantly, on September 8, 1875, Franklin and Ellen Miles became the parents of a son, Charles Franklin Miles. For a man who had missed family life for so long, the world must now have seemed a much different and better place.[5]

The next years were full to the brim. In 1876, in addition to his family and his medical practice, Miles took time for such activities as a debate before the Elkhart Literary Club, in which he defended Charles Darwin's theories.[6]

That year, too, he published his first known pamphlet: *A Popular Treatise on Diseases of the Ear; Deafness, Its Causes and Cure,* a 32-page booklet printed by the Mennonite Publishing Company of Elkhart. Miles aimed this work both toward the general public and toward other physicians. Placing faith in the public's ability to understand health matters, he vowed to avoid "all technicalities" in order to effectively reach them and correct some "crude and erroneous notions" about the ear and the effectiveness of popular but worthless remedies.

On the other hand, in some of his descriptions of treatments and use of case histories, he addressed the medical community, seeking, as physicians often did in this period by writing articles in medical journals, to attract referrals for "difficult and dangerous cases."[7]

His practice grew as he attracted "difficult and dangerous cases" from at least a modest radius around Elkhart. The *Elkhart Review* reported on his surgeries; for example, his uncrossing of the eyes of Ida and Emma Foegley of South Bend. He saw destitute patients with eye problems at county expense, as well as providing free treatment for some patients who could not afford to pay. In May, 1877, his business card in the *Review* announced a new office at the corner of Main Street and Jackson Boulevard, Elkhart's busiest intersection, over Browning's drugstore. He and his family lived in an adjoining apartment.[8]

In December, 1877, a reporter visited Miles' newly decorated office: " . . . the ceiling has been elegantly papered, the wood-work brightened up, and some easy chairs were scattered about, inviting one to 'sit down and make himself at home' before a cheery coal fire . . . the doctor, at the reporter's request, opened the depositories of his instruments, and for the first time he saw the delicate appliances used in the eye and ear practice. Keen-edged knives, slender probes, miniature glasses . . . "[9] In this welcoming setting, Miles worked toward making his patients' visits as pleasant as possible. And Ellen and the baby were always nearby.

The following year he added a large selection of eyeglasses, announcing the fact with an article in the *Review*. In "Facts Worth Remembering," he quoted eminent authorities on the need for prescription of glasses by a competent specialist. He wrote, "That I might avoid charging the customary fees, except in difficult cases, I was induced to purchase the largest and finest assortment of spectacles kept between Toledo and Chicago, consisting of French, English and American make. Have also made arrangement by which I frequently have spectacles, frames and lenses constructed to order (as is often necessary to obtain a fit) without added charge. I often have old frames set with new glasses, which are warranted to fit."[10]

For at least a short period, Ellen Miles joined her husband in medical practice. From November 1877 to April 1878, her business card was added to his in the *Review:* "Dr. Ellen D. Miles. Especial attention paid to Obstetrics and Diseases of Women."[11] However, family cares probably kept her from continuing. Their daughter Marian was born July 20, 1878, and their second daughter, Electa, was born in January, 1880.[12]

It is likely that Miles did not have much time away from his growing family and his medical practice. But he did pursue some other activities. In his office window, along with a case of spectacles, Miles displayed a small stuffed alligator. The specimen had recently been acquired by the Elkhart Museum Association, of which he was a founder and curator of archaeology.

Several of his fellow physicians joined him in collecting items for the museum. He brought relics of an Indian burial from the banks of the St. Joseph River; found a mastodon shoulder blade east of Mishawaka; contributed some artifacts and anatomical specimens; and added his father's Hawaiian shell collection, fossils, and mineral ores. The museum formally opened in August, 1880, in quarters over the city council room in the city hall.[13]

Notices in the newspapers also indicate that he enjoyed an occasional fishing outing. And he was appointed as an officer of the Royal Arcanum lodge, along with Dr. Frink and two of his future business partners, A. R. Burns and A. R. Beardsley.[14]

As time went on, his medical practice broadened. It was far from confined to his "specialty," and in fact his business card in the *Review* changed in 1878 to read simply, "Dr. F. Lawrence Miles, Physician & Surgeon." He brought discussions of a wide variety of cases to meetings of the Elkhart County Medical Association, an A.M.A. local affiliate which was organized in October, 1878. The Association met five times a year for the purpose of "promoting Harmony and Good Fellowship, and . . . elevating the Cause of Medicine and Collateral Sciences."

Among the cases Miles shared were "a case of typho malarial fever occurring in his own family," "a case of obstinate constipation," "a plan of placing children with high fevers in hammocks and gently swinging them wrapping first in a wet sheet if required," and "a case of Lead Poisoning occurring from the use of Flake white, treated with iodide of potassium successfully"; as well as cases related to his specialty, such as "a case of headache and sneezing caused entirely by glasses to correct for hypermetropia," "several cases of eye strain causing severe headaches," "a case of cataract-double operated on with complete success" and "bacteria in middle ear disease."[15]

The *Review* reported that he performed eye and ear surgery for patients from as far away as Chicago. One case involved creating an artificial pupil in the eye of a blind woman from Hillsdale, Michigan. But it also showed him involved with a colostomy, a burn case, and gallstones. Many a late night was spent traveling to his patients by horse and buggy over dirt roads.

Miles was actively responding to the health needs of his community. He furnished consultations at the request of fellow doctors, vaccinated the poor for smallpox without charge, and in 1880, served on Elkhart's fledgling municipal board of health.[16] This was a short-lived service, perhaps because Miles became involved in a bitter controversy with a politician.

In Elkhart, as in many towns and cities in this period, increasing contamination of well water combined with the usual proliferation of malarial insects in summer and fall to produce a high rate of bacterial disease. Especially prevalent were diphtheria and typhoid fever, as well as scarlet fever in winter. Two hundred cases of typhoid occurred in one year.

Unlike the dreaded smallpox, however, no control was possible since such cases were not required to be reported to the board of health. Elkhart's board consisted of Miles, B. F. Stephens (an undertaker) and J. R. Mather (a real estate developer). The board, probably at Miles' instigation, tried to change this, to ensure, in Miles' words, that "in addition to small-pox, which seldom causes a death in this city, scarlet and typhoid fevers, measles and diphtheria, each of which causes many deaths, also be reported to the Board, as is the case in neighboring States."

The board's proposal met defeat from the city council, because expense to the city promised to be greater. Councilman H. J. Kremer, who was defeated in the council elections that year, lashed out at Miles in the columns of the *Review,* accusing him of trying to get more public money for his services—to "suck at the public teat."

This attack struck a raw nerve in Miles. In a vitriolic exchange of letters in May, 1881, the two men traded insults, Kremer calling Miles an "infinitesimal M. D.," "little spectacle quack," and "little know-nothing, back-biting whiffet," Miles retaliating with "dead duck," "defunct councilman," "dead political trickster," "hypocritical steward," and "salary grabber." Shortly after their exchange the newly elected council appointed a new board of health which did not include Miles.[17]

4
Branching Out, 1881-1893

A Time of Trial

Both Franklin and Ellen Miles were ill in the summer of 1881. To try to recuperate, they retreated to Christiana Lake in nearby Cass County, Michigan, where Miles had gone on fishing expeditions. Franklin recovered; but on August 24, Ellen Miles died, at the age of thirty, "of the disease commonly called typho-malaria, aggravated by unusual bronchial and lung difficulties." In her obituary she was praised as "a most devoted wife and efficient helpmeet...never discontented, never sad, but ever lending the aid of a willing hand and a cheerful heart."[1]

Ellen Miles' death meant not only sadness and loss, but an increased burden for Franklin Miles. According to descendants, he insisted on keeping and raising the three children, aged eighteen months to six years, rather than sending them to a female relative, which might have been expected. He later told Louise Bass that he had kept them safe and warm at night by having one child sleep on each side of him, the third at the foot of the bed. Other descendants remember him as a loving and very strict parent who had high standards for his children, and later, grandchildren.[2]

One might think that such dedication to his family would have limited his activities. Yet the next few years saw the transformation of Franklin Miles from a busy medical practitioner into a medical entrepreneur and publicist/educator. He built a clinical and mail practice of thousands of patients, hiring assistants to help handle the load. He originated popular remedies which were sold throughout the United States. And he wrote and printed numerous pamphlets, covering many aspects of health and hygiene.

In so doing, like many other entrepreneur-physicians of his time, he would move away from complete acceptance by the emerging medical "establishment," violating the tenets of the code of ethics of the American Medical Association against self-advertising and the marketing of proprietary remedies. This process of change was completed in 1893, when he gave up his Elkhart practice and opened his "Medical and Ocular Institute" in Chicago.

He had long envisioned achieving a wider business influence with his scientific, legal and medical education. Now the time seemed right. His medical practice must have become burdensome. Competition from other physicians was growing. And the financial rewards were all too modest. Despite being busy with private and county patients, he attempted to increase his share of the medical market by holding weekly office hours in South Bend and by signing up as physician for the American Mutual Life Insurance Company in Elkhart.[3]

In addition, his work was wearing down his health. At one point, according to a biographical article, he was "given up to die of consumption—induced by close confinement and overwork—by three able physicians."[4] Though this was a mistaken prognosis, Miles' susceptibility to lung problems, such as pneumonia and bronchitis, would be a major factor in his later trips and move to Florida. It must certainly have reduced his ability to withstand the daily rigors of private practice, especially in the winter. He now sought to become less dependent upon it.[5]

"Have a Good Article"

The route to Miles' greater fame and prosperity would be the field of functional nervous disorders, of "neurasthenia," so recently opened up by Beard, Mitchell, and others. His new emphasis was evident in a newspaper advertisement in August, 1884: "Dr. Frank Lawrence Miles. Special attention paid Nervous Diseases, such as Sick and Nervous Headache, Dizziness, Neuralgia, Weak Eyes, Nervousness, Palpitation, Exhaustion, Epilepsy, etc. Spectacles fitted for medical purposes." This was a far cry from the simple business card of earlier years.[6]

His increasing work with nervous and chronic diseases was a combination of medical practice, research, invention, and entrepreneurship. He was convinced that the nerves and muscles of the eye, the nerve center at the base of the brain, and the autonomic nerves connecting the heart, stomach and other internal organs all affected each other and could be treated to remedy headache, nervous, heart and digestive disorders.

Keeping careful records of each case—following a recent trend in medical practice—he gave special emphasis to eye problems as a causative factor. Even where he found no visual defects that needed correction through eyeglasses, he found imbalances between muscles of the eye, which put a strain on the rest of the nervous system, in up to a quarter of his patients. To remedy this, he performed operations which corrected these imbalances, or prescribed special glasses.[7]

In 1884 he published an article in *The Weekly Medical Review of St. Louis* summarizing 115 cases in which eye conditions and improper glasses caused nasal problems.[8] He wrote Dr. Jewell at the *Journal of Nervous and Mental Diseases* about publishing more of his findings. "By all means publish your surprising results," Jewell replied, according to Miles' publications.[9]

By 1888 he had written five other informative pamphlets, including *Nervous Diseases, Permanent Cure of Headache Without Change of Occupation, Weak Eyes a Nervous Disease, Important Facts Concerning Headache and Other Nervous Diseases,* and *Use of Spectacles in Treatment of Afflictions of the Brain.*[10]

His interest in the design of eyeglasses also led him to invent an "Instrument for Measurement of Spectacles," patented in 1886, "capable of taking all the various measurements required for manufacturing a pair of spectacles to suit the individual."[11]

Early in this period of new emphasis on the nervous system came the development of his remedies. The first was Dr. Miles' Restorative Nervine, a liquid calmative he made from chemical ingredients. He began compounding it for patients who had symptoms of neurasthenic and other nervous conditions. He soon began thinking of marketing it commercially, and secured registration of the label from the U. S.

Patent Office on July 18, 1882. By October, he had made enough to distribute to local druggists.[12]

According to family and company tradition, Miles cooked the first batches of his Restorative Nervine in a wash boiler on a laundry stove in the family kitchen.[13] Though we have no exact knowledge of the original formula, the key ingredients seem to have been bromides of potassium, ammonia and sodium, blended with generous amounts of sugar.

The use of bromides was already well established, especially in the treatment of epilepsy, and the dangers of their overuse were being documented. According to a descendant, Miles included in Nervine a bit of Fowler's Solution (an arsenic preparation), which prevented or lessened a side effect of skin rash.[14]

In "uncomplicated" conditions, such as simple exhaustion, Dr. Miles' Restorative Nervine often relieved the problem completely. In hundreds of testimonials printed in Miles' publications over the next few years, users of Nervine testified to its effectiveness in relieving insomnia, restoring appetite, and getting them through periods of extreme nervousness and exhaustion. In later conversations with his daughter, Miles spoke especially of the many farm wives he had treated who were worn out by headaches, worry and overwork.[15]

In more complex cases, Miles advertised his Nervine, and the other preparations he developed, as elements in a complete system of treatment. In an 1893 pamphlet he classified his remedies thus: "1st. remedies to remove the weakness or disease of the affected organ; 2nd. to remove all exciting or sympathetic causes or complications; 3rd. to give temporary relief while the patient is being permanently cured." Among these temporary measures he classed "the use of opiates, bromides, antipyrine, or other palliative remedies," and thus, Nervine.[16]

In developing his own remedies for sale, Miles was responding to the shortage of effective, reliable drugs available to physicians. Medicine now recognized the need to treat each case with a precise combination of specific chemical drugs; but creation of effective preparations lagged far behind. Since the public demanded medicines, the void had long been filled by a confusing array of secret-formula patent medicines, as well as by potent, dangerous drugs which were a holdover from the years of "heroic medicine."

Proprietary medicine by this time was a crowded field, with many additional firms entering the ranks after the repeal of certain federal taxes in 1883. The manufacturers vied in the pages of newspapers, in various forms of outdoor advertising, and in company literature which deluged the counters of drugstores and general stores. It was, in fact, the booming patent medicine industry that fostered the growth of the advertising agency as a business in the post-Civil War period.[17]

In the unregulated world of proprietary medicine there were many charlatans, giving the entire field a clouded reputation. Miles did not want to be classed with these charlatans. He identified himself in his advertising as a practicing physician and medical researcher who delegated the manufacture and sale of his remedies to qualified businessmen. "Dr. Miles," said one of his pamphlets, *"is not a patent medicine man."*[18]

Miles was not a charlatan. Most of the remedies he developed were made up of ingredients currently favored by reputable physicians. Formulas were never disclosed; yet he sought not only to control the quality of his products but also to maintain a personal responsibility to those who used them.

He refused to promote his remedies as cure-alls, and stayed away from advocating them for acute or terminal sicknesses. Thus he avoided one of the worst evils of proprietary medicine makers in that era: promoting false hopes and promising a cure when none was possible.

But he did strive for wide distribution and influence, and to some extent availed himself of the less scrupulous patent medicine makers' promotional methods. It should not be surprising that he would be branded with their label.

No doubt he was spurred in his efforts by the entrepreneurial environment of Elkhart, as well as by the huge success of the patent medicine industry in general. In the 1870s and 1880s he saw Herbert Bucklen, son of Isaac Bucklen, a pioneer druggist and neighbor of his father in Civil War days, rise to wealth as the proprietor of "Dr. King's New Discovery" and "Arnica Salve." The A. N. Chamberlain Medicine Co. had made "Immediate Relief" in Elkhart for years. And in 1883 Elkhart druggist John P. Primley and M. S. A. Jones began making chewing gum and patent medicines; two years later they built a three-story factory.[19]

None of these men were doctors; none had Miles' detailed knowledge of human physiology. He did not believe that such people should be allowed to monopolize the field.

In being "more than" a patent medicine maker, it was important to Miles that his advertising also incorporate his professional credentials, theories, and educational advice concerning health care, all delivered in a readable style that would, as Chesterfield would advise, guard against pedantry, and reflect the interests of his readers.

His account book shows that packets of "Journals," no doubt describing the nervous system, accompanied the first distribution of Nervine in 1882. And his first mention of the name "Miles Medical Co." in March, 1884 was followed very shortly by the publication of *The Medical News.* It was a journal, according to the *Review,* "he purposes to issue regularly. It is intended to give an epitome of the later discoveries in certain lines of medical science, and will at the same time contain departments devoted to special topics, as The Household, The Children, etc. The Dr. will use it quite largely to advertise his remedies." According to company records, this publication was sent out in revised editions for a number of years.[20]

Again, the Elkhart business climate may have spurred his undertaking publications of this kind. In the 1870s and 1880s, two prominent Elkhart figures were achieving wide influence through publishing. Charles G. Conn, the nation's largest manufacturer of brass musical instruments, achieved fame with the help of his musical journal, known at various times as *Trumpet Notes, Conn's Truth,* and *Conn's Musical Truth.* And the Rev. John F. Funk reached Mennonites throughout the world with his *Herald of Truth,* issued in both English and German. Especially for a man who could not be at the nation's power centers, printer's ink was an important way to nationwide influence and success.

Birth of a Company; Medicine by Mail

The production and marketing of Nervine remained very modest as long as Miles was doing it himself. In the years 1882-84, distribution was limited to some two dozen druggists in Elkhart and surrounding counties in northern Indiana and southern Michigan. Miles' account book showed a total of seven dozen bottles distributed in 1882, thirty-one dozen in 1883, and twenty-five dozen in 1884.[21]

Accompanying these were copies of the "News," "journals," "pamphlets," "circulars," and "letters," totalling about 10,000 in 1882, 19,000 in 1883, and 9,000 in 1884. According to a story passed on by Jack Linton of Elkhart, David New, a rural resident, chatted with Miles as he personally delivered his remedy and literature in a two-horse phaeton. Miles, he recalled, was looking for partners to enlarge the business.[22]

The next year, Miles did find two partners, Hugh McLachlan and Norris Felt, proprietors of The Fair, a drygoods store on Elkhart's Main Street. Each man put $500 into the enterprise, which was incorporated as the Dr. Miles Medical Company on October 28, 1885. The articles of incorporation listed four remedies, all part of his system of treatment: Dr. Miles' Restorative Nervine, Dr. Miles' Restorative Nerve & Liver Pills, Dr. Miles' Restorative Tonic, and Dr. Miles' Restorative Blood Purifier.[23]

The Nerve and Liver Pill was a laxative that, in Miles' words, "regulates and strengthens the stomach, liver and bowels." Trademark for the Nerve and Liver Pill was obtained in 1887. According to much later records, the pills contained extract of aloin, ipecac and podophyllin. The Restorative Tonic, which, Miles wrote, "builds up the system and removes the debility resulting from nervous and other chronic diseases," contained three ingredients very heavily used in Miles' day—iron, quinine and alcohol—blended with sugar.

The Blood Purifier was designed "for removing impurities of the blood, such as Scrofula, Skin Diseases, Syphilis, etc., which often affect the brain and nervous system." As later revealed, it combined potassium iodide and Fowler's Solution with some seven plant extracts.[24]

At the first stockholders' meeting, the three directors, Miles, Felt and McLachlan, agreed to label every bottle as follows: "As diseases are sometimes complicated and as the nature and constitution of people are not always precisely alike, it must be acknowledged by every honest and sensible person that the very best medicine in the world cannot completely cure in every case. Therefore, those using Dr. Miles' remedies without being entirely cured, are earnestly requested to notify him in person or by letter, that he may give all necessary advice without charge.

"Again, it is the Christian duty of every person greatly benefited to inform Dr. Miles, that the truth may be known and other fellow sufferers likewise cured." One-third of the revenues from all such cases referred by the company to Dr. Miles were to be turned over by him to the company—indicating that the "advice without charge" was to be followed up, if possible, by paid treatment.[25]

This "disclaimer," which would bring in many testimonials and help form the basis of Miles' personal practice of medicine by mail, shows the close relationship between his medical practice and private research on one hand, and his sending of remedies "out into the world" on the other. He plainly wanted to establish a doctor-patient relationship with the unseen users of his remedies. He wanted to maintain a sense of responsibility for the effectiveness of his medications. And he wanted to gather information on their cases for his growing research files, as well as potent "ammunition" for his advertising.

The new medical company grew slowly in its first two years, moving to new quarters at least twice, in December 1885 and January 1887, and adding some forty new customers.[26] A partial reorganization in February, 1887, however, changed things considerably. Felt and McLachlan's interests were purchased by A. R. Burns, a forty-five-year-old Elkhart druggist, and George Compton, a thirty-seven-year-old mill owner. In later writings, Miles referred to this new partnership as the start of the firm.

According to the *Review*, Burns "took an active hand in the management" of the company. He also helped compound the medicines and deliver orders to druggists. Compton, the son of a pioneer farmer of Osolo Township, Elkhart County, served as treasurer. Family recollections trace his interest in joining the firm to his wife, Elizabeth Ames Compton, whom Miles had cured of headaches. It is said that she helped persuade Miles to form a company to manufacture his remedies.[27]

Production was now increased. Women were hired to package the medicine. Salesmen were sent out with medicine and literature to widen interest. Newspaper advertising was begun in Indiana, Illinois, and Ohio.[28] An important new product was added to the line: Dr. Miles' New Cure, registered with the U. S. Patent Office in 1887. The New Cure was designed to regulate and strengthen the heart. As later described, it contained an extract of cactus grandiflorus (made from cactus shipped from Mexico), combined with extract of digitalis, alcohol and other ingredients. Later it was known as Cactus Compound.[29] In March, 1888, the company moved to the former office of the *Elkhart Independent* on West High Street, and by the following year had added customers in seven states.[30]

In 1889, the company made a major advance toward the strong, self-sufficient business management Miles desired. A second reorganization brought into the company's ownership and management forty-year-old Albert R. Beardsley, a successful businessman and member of Elkhart's most prominent pioneer family.[31] Albert R. Beardsley and his nephew, Andrew Hubble ("Hub") Beardsley, who joined the firm the following year, would expand the small company into a nationally recognized leader in the proprietary medicine industry. And they would make it possible for Dr. Miles to distance himself more and more into an advisory role.

Advertising, sales effort and manufacturing all increased rapidly under the Beardsleys' leadership. By 1892 there were over fifty employees, and the company had moved into its own new, spacious, three-story building on West Franklin Street.[32] Miles also promoted the idea that the company should have its own complete printing plant. An addition (the first of several) was built for this purpose shortly thereafter.[33]

Miles, who would keep the title of president until 1928, would continue to be extremely important to the company, though in an advisory capacity—and the company to him. His knowledge of chemistry and medicine were needed for its success; his name and authoritative voice were vital to its advertising and labeling. Early publications of the firm, in turn, advertised Miles' own practice; and in late 1890 the directors (including Miles), seeing the company begin to make a profit, voted to pay him royalties for the past three years on all drugs sold: the tidy sum of $5.00 per dozen on all bottled medicines (each bottle retailed for $1.00) and $1.00 per dozen boxes of pills.[34]

Miles gave even more of his attention, however, to the challenges of his growing private clinic, which broadened to include dispensing advice and medications through the mail. By June 1891, perhaps aided by the royalties from the medical company, he had moved his clinic into large new quarters on the second floor of the Nickless Block at the corner of Main and Pratt Streets.

The *Review* reported, "He occupies the entire floor, something over a hundred feet deep, and has a series of offices, or rooms, connecting with each other by means of double doors, extending nearly the whole length. The reception room is in the front, the Doctor's private room next, correspondence room back of this, then his drug room, next a spectacle room and at the extreme eastern end, the packing room."[35]

His mail practice grew partly out of inquiries received through the medical company, and partly from personal advertising efforts. It was aimed primarily at people in rural areas and small towns, who often had no access to competent medical care, or even to any medical care at all. Bearing some resemblance to his plans, years ago, for "scientific propagation" questionnaires, self-examination charts now were at the heart of his mail practice. People living in the remotest corners of America, even outside it, could fill out a lengthy form detailing their symptoms and medical history, and receive back medical advice.

Their case records were placed alongside those of his other patients in Miles' fast-growing files. The expansion of the mail business required hiring additional assistants, such as clerks and stenographers. Little is known of the medications he dispensed and mailed from his clinic in this period, where they came from or how closely related they were to the products of the medical company. In 1883, he registered the label for a preparation called Dr. Miles' Great Remedy—a name never used by the company—with the U. S. Patent Office.[36]

Among his assistants he employed Miss Elizabeth State, who first worked in 1889 for the medical company, then as his office clerk; and finally, after special training, as an optician for the clinic. A petite, attractive, vivacious young woman some twenty years younger than Miles, she had come to Elkhart with her Irish-born parents about 1870. Elizabeth State quickly won Franklin Miles' admiration and, after a period of several years, would become his second wife.[37]

For the present, however, his personal life in the 1880s and early 1890s seems to have revolved mostly around his family of three growing children, and his Elkhart "cronies." For relaxation, he pitched quoits on summer evenings with A. R. Burns and a few others in the rear of the Nickless block. And he was an active participant in the Elkhart Sportsmen's Club, also known as the Christiana Club, a men's fishing group which had its clubhouse at Christiana Lake and sponsored spirited contests. In one day, he and a friend caught 80 bass.[38]

Growing Power in Print

In his writings of the late 1880s and early 1890s, Miles continued to try to educate the public in health matters, as well as advertising aggressively. He also spoke out on some vital issues. *Human Rights* ("A Quarterly Journal for the People, Devoted to the Physical, Mental and Moral Improvement of the Human Race"), which he issued in

April, 1888 as his own, rather than a company publication, is a remarkable document. It further elaborated the theme of "scientific propagation" and expressed his outrage as an educated man, parent and physician against the ignorance, excesses and social abuses of his time.

He opened by praising "Progress" in his own poem ("from a New York Weekly"), progress which triumphed despite encounters with "human wolves" and "sharks." But city-dwellers were in danger of becoming "extinct," he maintained, citing J. Milner Fothergill (an English physician), because of terrible health habits: "intemperance, deficient exercise, lack of fresh air and sunlight, over brain work, too rich and indigestible food, want of sleep, injurious styles of dress, a constant cultivation of the mind and almost total neglect of the body," in Fothergill's words.[39]

Next, Miles took up the cause of "Children's Rights." "While there are *Thirty-Three* societies for the prevention of cruelty to *Animals* in the United States," he wrote, "we have heard of not one formed for the prevention of cruelty to *children*." He compared the American child mortality rate unfavorably to that of livestock. He contrasted American ignorance with British wisdom in child-rearing practices.

In "Children's Rights vs Parental Empiricism," he again decried child mortality, enumerating some of its causes and concluding that "as breeders of swine, men may be termed scientists; as parents, the grossest of empirics."[40] He reminded his readers of the poor sanitary conditions at Elkhart's schools; just a few months earlier, he had organized a society in Elkhart "for the promotion of physical culture," with an emphasis on education in matters of child-raising and sanitation.[41]

Under "Rights of Youths," Miles accused schools of placing "higher value on the ornamental than on the useful in education," neglecting especially to teach the laws of health. State boards of education, he claimed, would not make changes because they were dominated by "bookworms." (Chesterfield too had cautioned to beware of them.) Every such board, Miles believed, should contain a physician, a statesman and a clergyman.[42]

In "Rights of the Citizen," Miles attacked "Giant Monopolies for

Robbing the Poor," including the Standard Oil Trust, the Steel Beam Trust and many others. He concluded that "there is not a person in the land who does not almost daily pay tribute to some band of robbers, who live in luxury, while many of their victims can not obtain the necessities of life for themselves and illy nourished and clothed children." Citizens had the right to be protected, not only from them, but from foreign immigration and adulterated food.[43]

In "Rights of the Race" he would establish controls on human breeding, including "the right to have those desiring to marry examined as to their physical, intellectual and moral fitness to assume the great responsibility of parentage." He claimed, in accord with much current thinking, that pauperism and alcoholism as well as retardation and insanity were hereditary and that such people should not be allowed to marry.[44]

"The Art of Prolonging Life" led to a discussion of diseases of the heart and nervous system. Rather than going on to advertise his services, however, Miles gave the formulas for several prescriptions from famous physicians, which readers could presumably take to their druggists to be compounded.[45]

Human Rights was only one of a succession of "popular magazines" which had begun with *The Medical News.* A second, expanded issue, *Human Rights, or How to Succeed,* followed a few months later, featuring a biographical sketch of P. T. Barnum. Not the magazine, but some of Miles' correspondence from Barnum, has survived. This may have been the journal described by the *Review* as a "proposed medical journal" for "popular medical information and instruction," to be edited by local writer O. Z. Hubbell. [46]

Pamphlets written for the company were equally full of opinion and advice, and equally unafraid of controversy. Increasingly, they showed him both eliciting and reacting to criticism from the medical community. *New and Startling Facts for Those Afflicted With Nervous Diseases,* dating to about 1891, gave a full exposition of Miles' "restorative system," under the heading, "The Acme of Medical Genius." It also featured detailed articles on nervous and heart disease and plentiful advice on hygiene, including warnings against tea, coffee, alcohol and tobacco, and tight corsets.[47]

In the course of its forty pages he quoted Jewell, Beard, and many other medical authorities, but claimed some original discoveries. In later writings, Miles would indicate that his theories were not accepted by the medical world until years afterward.

Protesting against the "no-advertising" standard of physicians, he wrote, "It has long been the practice of ignorant and unscrupulous persons to advertise single remedies to cure all the ills to which man is subject. However, a moment's reflection will make clear to any unprejudiced mind, that it is wrong to permit ignorant and dishonest men to have the sole use of so extensive and powerful a means for good or evil as printer's ink.

"No one will deny that it is manifestly wrong for learned and conscientious specialists to hide their light under the bushel of popular or professional prejudice, when by letting it shine before men, they may be the means of saving much misery to their fellowman and thus greatly lessening the number of unfortunate victims of these human sharks."

"Had it not been for considerations of this nature," he continued, "Dr. Miles would never have placed his System of Remedies into the hands of a company of honorable and energetic capitalists for the purpose of placing them within the reach of persons, who owing to distance, lack of time or money, could not consult him personally, and who, more than likely, never would have heard of him..."[48]

In a prominent article, Miles cautioned his readers to beware of "sharks in human form" (unscrupulous imitators) and druggists with cheap remedies that are "just as good."[49]

In contrast to the pamphlet's quite substantial body of information and rather dignified stance, its arresting style of typography and illustration seemed designed to "startle" the reader and perhaps cause unwarranted alarm. Boldface type on every page made key phrases stand out, such as "BLEEDING," "INSTANT OR SPEEDY DEATH," "FATAL MISTAKES," "GOLDEN OPPORTUNITIES," or "FREE." Well-placed drawings depicted grimacing, falling and prostrate people.

In this and subsequent publications such as *The Family Physician* (1891-92) and *Modern Miracles* (1892-93), there were many testimonials, sometimes accompanied by engravings of patients' faces and bold, arresting headlines. All of the succeeding company publications, and some of those Miles issued on behalf of the clinic, would be in this "patent medicine" style, typical of the proprietary industry of the time. The company's growing sales proved their effectiveness.

It was just these sorts of publications, whether or not they came from reputable men, printed by the millions and given out to the public in drugstores, that were seen as threatening by physicians. It was not only that the products and medical authorities they touted were unknown quantities, but also that their plentiful medical advice and systems of treatment seemed to render the local physician unnecessary. In this period, in fact, a few of the most prominent physicians were beginning scattered attacks on proprietary manufacturers that would later become a well-organized campaign.[50]

Without question, Miles had begun to alienate himself from the medical community, especially from some of its more advanced critics of the patent medicine business. Dr. E. F. Ingals of Rush Medical College, later a trustee of the American Medical Association, was disturbed enough by Miles' practices to make an entry in the old Rush matriculation book of 1874, next to Miles' name: "Quack of the worst sort. By the order of Dr. E. F. Ingals June 1892."[51]

But it was typical of Miles that suspicion and opposition only made him work harder and aim higher. In *Modern Miracles,* he appealed to the public for testimonials which he would publish to refute "selfish" doctors who were "taking steps to have laws passed in the different states to stop the sale of all such medicines, which 'injure their practice.'"[52]

And he had grand plans for his clinic, including a move to Chicago. Ever since medical school, the city's possibilities had beckoned. One of the main centers of American medicine, Chicago was the home of many prominent physicians and the headquarters of the American Medical Association.

Defying opposition from other medical men, Miles visualized a large and successful clinic, bringing him cases from far and wide, perhaps a bit like Mitchell's in Philadelphia, where assistant physicians supplied additional specialties. Chicago also provided an ideal location from which to address the far-off patient who needed his advice and "personal treatment" by mail.

A move would make it possible for him to escape the relatively backward conditions of Elkhart and to leave behind his long-standing Elkhart medical practice, which was still onerous. In 1890, for example, he had treated the eyes of one of his county patients 192 times, and performed an operation, for a total fee of $37.00. In another case, where the patient seemed incurable, he had charged nothing at all.[53]

Now that the medical company was on a firm footing, too, he could confidently distance himself still more from it as well. There is some possibility, in fact, that as long as he was in Elkhart, his dispensing separate medications on behalf of the clinic may have caused discomfort or confusion on the part of the company managers. In Chicago, he would feel freer to develop his own operation.[54]

There is no evidence, however, that his move was meant to be permanent and irrevocable. Miles' movements over the next few years would show him repeatedly being drawn back to Elkhart by strong ties of business, family and friendship.

Dr. Franklin L. Miles, ca. 1885-1890.

Electa Lawrence Miles, mother of Dr. Franklin Miles.

Ellen Lighthall Miles, first wife of Dr. Miles.

Photo of Dr. Miles Medical Co. building on Franklin St. near
S.E. corner of Second, ca. 1892.

Elizabeth State, Miles' second wife, in
1889.

5
Wealth, 1893-1906

The Tallest Office Building in the World

In 1893, all eyes were on Chicago, site of the World's Columbian Exposition; and it seems appropriate that an ambitious Elkhart medical man would choose this moment to enter the commercial and medical "hub." Miles and his son and two daughters, now in their teens, found a house in the new and fashionable Hyde Park area, whose development had been much accelerated by the Exposition.[1]

He found office space for his "Medical and Ocular Institute" on the thirteenth floor of the Masonic Temple Building at the northwest corner of State and Randolph Streets. At twenty-four stories, it was the tallest office building in the world; some 8,000 people traveled up to its dome each day for a view of the city. A number of other physicians also had offices there.[2]

Miles soon had printed an elaborate brochure with four-color cover describing the "Institute."[3] According to its portrayal of the new clinic's personnel and services, he aimed for a wider scope than in Elkhart, and showed sensitivity to the new emphasis in medicine on scientific laboratory techniques which was replacing the "empiric" skills of the old-time physician.[4]

The Institute, to be staffed by "Many Assistant Physicians, Business Manager, Opticians, Stenographers, Typewriters, Prescription Clerks, etc.," would offer five departments: "Special Treatment of Chronic Diseases of the Brain, Nerves and Heart," "Special Treatment of Chronic Nasal, Throat and Lung Diseases," "Treatment of Diseases of the Liver, Stomach and Bowels," "Special Treatment of Diseases, Weaknesses and Deformities of the Eye," and "Scientific Fitting of Spectacles in Difficult Cases, and in the Treatment of Nervous Diseases."[5]

Respiratory problems were to be handled by a "competent specialist," recently returned from London, using "all the most modern apparatus." Kidney and venereal disease would be diagnosed through analysis of the urine, by an "analyst and microscopist" of many years' experience, trained in the United States and Europe. Treatments were offered through the mail for women's diseases and skin diseases; the brochure said Miles had a new treatment for skin disease "very much in advance of any of the ordinary methods," and that remedies for uterine diseases had been developed in the course of treating spinal irritations.

In the midst of all this, the figure of Dr. Miles was pre-eminent. The bearded physician, pictured several times in the pamphlet, continued to personally treat "difficult cases," examining a patient's eyes with his apparatus, and doing surgeries in his small Victorian operating room. Miles, who advertised his own and the Institute's services in the *Chicago Blue Book,* associated with him Dr. William J. Beeman, an 1885 graduate of Chicago Medical College. It is very likely, too, that Elizabeth State accompanied him to Chicago as one of his two "experienced opticians."[6]

In this pamphlet, perhaps for the first time, Miles described the "symptom blanks" which his corresponding patients were to fill out and send to the Institute. "The most timid person or one whose mind acts slowly," he wrote, "can describe their case in writing much more readily and accurately than in the presence of a strange physician or new surroundings."[7]

The patient form furnished a detailed, permanent record, one which most other physicians did not have time to keep. This system must have appealed strongly not only to Miles the promoter, but to Miles the rationalist. Why, he must have reasoned, could not untrained but literate people accurately describe their own symptoms, if given a form that was detailed enough?

In his booklet, too, Miles christened as "Miles' Disease" those functional nervous afflictions involving the head, eyes, heart and stomach, such as sick headache and palpitations, caused by irritation of the nerve centers at the base of the brain and upper part of the spine. A long list of satisfied patients was included.[8] For epilepsy, Miles offered his "Special Treatment." According to a later analysis, this preparation may have been somewhat akin to the company's Restorative Nervine.[9]

As proprietor of a medical organization which offered so many services, as a physician who claimed to base his practice on scientific research, and as president and "physician in chief" of a fast-growing medical company, Miles asserted his right to a position of leadership. This included spirited efforts to reply to "envious detractors."

In return, he attacked some physicians' practices of advertising without seeming to be advertising, such as operating their own hospitals and free clinics, and strategically placing journals and article reprints; and at the same time criticizing him for "openly and manfully" telling the public of his experience.[10]

In 1895, Miles published another description of his clinic in a book entitled *A New Era Dawning* in *Medical Science*. In it he summarized his findings to date concerning the nervous system, pressing especially the analogy to an electrical system, in which the various parts must be inspected and repaired. He gave a long exposition of his mail treatment plan, complete with lists of customers, state by state, and testimonials listed under types of "illustrative cases."

That his Institute, which he now had renamed the Miles Medical Association, met with some success is evident from his claim that his conclusions were now based on records of over 30,000 patient case studies. "These records," Dr. Miles wrote, "when placed one upon the other form a column thirty feet high."[11]

Meanwhile, as "physician in chief" of the Dr. Miles Medical Co., Miles continued to play an important role in regard to its products and advertising, though at a clear distance. This is shown in a rare letter, preserved in the Miles Archives, from Miles to the company's managers on March 17, 1894. He noted that the company's advertising writer and artist had spent a good deal of time with him in his Chicago office, discussing Miles' "copy" and "instructions" for a new company "paper."

Miles also had received a proof of a Nervine newspaper advertisement for approval. He suggested that all such ads should include a reference to his experience as a specialist, and to the availability of *Startling Facts*. To accentuate his point, he wrote, "Both Green and Paine harp on the discoverer of their remedies in nearly every one of their ads." He also believed in large advertisements, saying, "one of our small ads in a paper containing their larger ads is simply *thrown away.*"[12]

Though the tone of the letter suggests that Miles did not have total control over the style and content of the company's advertising, the company's literature for several years continued to carry his distinctive stamp. Styled to look like magazines or newspapers, the illustrated publications bore such titles as *The Doctor, Dr. Miles' Medical Monthly, Famous Men and Women, The Heart-The Human Engine, Short Talks with Dr. Franklin Miles LL.B., The Sunshine of Good Health Is Better Than Gold or Silver, Dr. Miles' Nervine Restored Our Health,* and *Dr. Miles' Prize Puzzle.*

In these publications, less and less space was devoted to treatise-like description, and more and more to testimonials. Patients, rather than notables of medicine, were the true authorities for the company's readers. These testimonials were supplemented by appealing articles on subjects of general interest. The importance of advertising in the company's activity is incontestable: in late 1895, the *Review* reported the company had spent over a million dollars on advertising in the past five years.[13]

Miles contributed one major new product to the company's line in these years. The Dr. Miles' Anti-Pain Pill, introduced in 1893, reportedly at the World's Columbian Exposition, was based on acetanilid, then one of the most-favored drugs for reducing fever as well as substituting for more addictive painkillers. Later in the decade, the company introduced some minor items: Dr. Miles' Nerve Plasters, Dr. Miles' Cold Cure, and Dr. Miles' Wine of Sasparilla.[14]

With his legal training, Miles was very much aware of the law as it pertained to drug manufacture, limited as that law was at the time. In 1897 he recommended, and the company's board approved, the removal of strychnine from Nervine, Heart Cure, and Anti-Pain Pills, in accordance with the "Wisconsin Law."[15]

In a postscript to his 1894 letter, Miles made the remark, "I shall hereafter expect remuneration for all work done for the Miles Medical Co. I cannot afford longer to devote my time to their service without pay, especially as they have seen fit to charge me for all services they render."[16]

Plainly, Miles felt that company matters were taking up too much of his time. But the financial rewards of company ownership and service soon became substantial for Miles and his fellow stockholders. In 1894, the success of the company was such that the directors voted a dividend of $4.00 per share, to be issued as often as funds warranted. In 1895, they added a monthly salary for all officers of the corporation.

The amounts were raised periodically, and for the rest of his life, Miles would receive thousands of dollars each month from the company. In addition, in 1894-95 Miles made two loans to the company at five per cent interest, and the company's cash books recorded what seem to have been special payments of "Bills-Dr. Miles" of some $37,000.[17]

A Wealth of Involvements

The balance of Miles' interests and activities began to change somewhat as the century's end approached. Medicine and the criticisms of the medical world began to be a little less all-important; there was more room to pursue friendships, family life, social and political concerns. Though always remaining active as head of his clinic and as president and advisor to the medical company, he slowed the pace of his research, development of new products, and output of new publications, and more or less stopped seeing patients personally.

It was a time of growing richness in Miles' personal life. He had developed a number of friendships in his Elkhart years, and no friend was closer than Col. Cyrus Roys (1836-1915), a prominent lawyer and writer, who spent much of his time in Elkhart during eighteen years as attorney for the Lake Shore & Michigan Southern Railroad.

Roys' wife was Katherine Morehous, daughter of Philo Morehous, an Elkhart pioneer banker who had helped bring the railroad, and growth, to Elkhart. While based in Chicago, Roys served as president of the Union League Club. He later retired to Elkhart and pursued a career of lecturing, writing, and world travel. Katherine Roys' sister Frances Morehous Stevens and her family completed a family group to which Franklin Miles was very close.

In Cyrus Roys, Miles found someone with intellectual interests as keen as his own, whose age and experience of life as an officer in the Civil War gave him a slight superiority, and who shared Miles' love of nature and passion for fishing. His mind, according to a biographical sketch, was a good match for Miles': "direct, straightforward and severely logical," with "a remarkable memory and a fine sense of humor."

Like Miles, Roys was liberal in his religious views. As a man of equal intelligence, in a non-competitive field, to whom Miles might unburden himself, he was the sort of friend Chesterfield would have recommended.[18]

In this period, too, came Miles' marriage to Elizabeth State, on July 17, 1895. In the early years of their association, according to Miles' remarks to his daughter Louise, Miles had kept his distance, believing she should be given ample opportunity to "find" a younger man. Now they entered into what was to be a most propitious and happy marriage.

With her sociable temperament and delight in entertaining, Elizabeth was the ideal partner for Franklin. Since they had worked together some six years, she knew him so well that she was attuned to every nuance of his personality. She was well known also to Miles' children, who were about ten to fifteen years younger. They enjoyed her cheerful disposition and love of telling stories.[19]

Sadness, however, came not long after this happy event. Elizabeth gave birth to a daughter, Frances, who was partially paralyzed and throughout the nearly nine years of her life could never walk or speak. Miles later told Louise that Frances' condition was the result of having been dropped by a nurse shortly after birth.

That her parents loved and accepted Frances is indicated by a family recollection that Miles designed a special chair which made it possible for her to move around the house. Yet it is likely that they had full-time help in her care, for they were extremely active in these years.[20]

Political issues increasingly drew Miles' interest. An early indication of this was his 1895 "campaign" on behalf of the support of Cuban insurgency. In his 1895 "popular magazine," *Success,* he wrote, "There is a heartlessness in successful business that must be compensated for by large charities in some other field, or else the highly successful man must after all remain the most unsuccessful of all men."[21]

In the fall of 1895, American indignation at the Spanish regime in Cuba was at fever pitch. In September, citizens of Chicago, holding mass meetings with insurgent representatives, were ready to send regiments to Cuba to aid the rebels. Miles became involved, and the Beardsleys did as well.

On Sept. 20, the company began mailing a circular and blank petition entitled "Shall Cuba Be Free?" throughout the country, a hundred thousand copies or more, asking all who believed Cuba should be free of Spain to sign and return them to the company.[22]

A few days later, the *Elkhart Review* praised the company for "awakening" the people, including those of Elkhart. Petitions were being signed in the "hotel offices, reading rooms and prominent places of business about our own city." At the medical company, the writer saw "heaps of correspondence," including letters from mayors, doctors, lawyers, manufacturers, prominent clergymen, and editors from all over the country.[23]

In December, Miles, representing "the Cuban sympathizers committee and movement," personally delivered the petitions, containing 92,200 names, to Illinois' Rep. Royce in Washington. Royce introduced a resolution in Congress calling for a "speedy recognition of the Cuban patriots."[24]

The next spring, Miles would have the satisfaction of seeing Congress pass a Cuban insurgency resolution, but the disappointment of seeing President Cleveland do little about it. That year, Miles, the Beardsleys, and his circle of family and friends all worked for the election of William McKinley—favored, no doubt, both for his pro-Cuban and financial platforms.

In August, the company mailed to every newspaper in which it advertised a request that a clause be added to the yearly contract, giving the company the right to cancel its contract if Bryan were elected. "Very few," reported the *Review*, "refuse to do so."[25] In Elkhart, Cyrus Roys and James H. State, Elizabeth's brother and a respected lawyer, gave campaign addresses. On February 27, 1897, the *Review* reported that Miles, A. R. Beardsley and A. H. Beardsley would be among those representing the medical company at McKinley's inauguration in Washington.[26]

Back and Forth

In the spring of 1897, Franklin and Elizabeth made the first of their two "returns" to Elkhart. In early May, the *Review* reported that Miles was moving his office furniture to the "Gillette Block, in rooms recently vacated by Dodge and Hubbell"—his old quarters at 401 South Main. He also maintained a Chicago office at 1317 Masonic Temple building in his own name, rather than that of the Dr. Miles Medical Association.[27]

Not a great deal is known of the clinic's activities in this period, except that in 1899 there were at least six principal employees, including Dr. Beeman. Miles probably employed additional women to aid in the correspondence and wrapping and mailing of medicines.[28]

First renting the home of J. B. Davenport at 24 Jackson Blvd., then living on Second Street, the Miles gave much attention to social and political activities. Miles and Roys were charter members of the new Century Club, a men's club made up of Elkhart's elite.[29] In June,

1898, Miles was a delegate to the district Republican convention at Rochester, working (unsuccessfully) for Roys' nomination for Congress.

The Miles home was the scene of creatively conceived parties. In May, 1898, they entertained forty guests using a patriotic theme, giving out favors of red, white and blue. In November that year, Miles hosted fifty male friends for dinner and pedro (a card game), supplying each guest with "a souvenir appropriate to his character or calling." There were waitresses, footmen, and musicians.[30]

With the lessening of his private practice at the clinic, Miles freed himself and his family to travel, and this too became one of his enthusiasms. The first mention of a winter trip to Florida came in the *Review* in December 1895; others followed, removing Miles at least briefly from the northern winters which were so hard on his lungs. A few years later, there would be a trip to Europe.[31]

In May, 1899, the *Review* announced that the Miles family and the Dr. Franklin Miles Medical Association were returning to Chicago. "When the doctor moved his office to Elkhart from Chicago two years ago," said the paper, "he undertook to ascertain whether he could do as well with headquarters here, as he desired to make his home in Elkhart, but extensive experiments and observations have shown that the prestige of Chicago's name brought much larger returns." His "office force" of six associates accompanied Miles to the new headquarters on the southeast corner of State and Adams Streets.[32]

Time bore out Miles' judgement, for the Association, which had now added the name "Grand Dispensary," became large and successful in the next few years. By January, 1902, there was "a large and carefully trained staff" of associate physicians, and "forty other assistants - pharmacists, chemists, statisticians, etc., who are in the analytical, in the microscopical, statistical and therapeutic departments." His operation was "four times as large as any other similar one in Chicago or New York."[33]

Miles now sent his patients-by-correspondence four "Copyrighted Examination Charts" which gave "four different and distinct views of each case...a veritable cross examination."[34] His 1902 booklet, *Dr. Miles'*

Neuropathic Cure for Diseases of the Heart, Lungs, Stomach, Liver, Kidneys and Nerves, contained recommendations from a number of publications. They joined the inevitable testimonials in reiterating his knowledge, skill and scientific methods, designed to win public confidence. One article, reprinted from *The Farm, Field and Fireside*, described his clinic:

"From the moment the visitor enters the handsome reception room and is met by the smiling attendant without a moment's delay, until, his wants properly attended to, he takes his departure, he cannot fail to be impressed with the perfect smoothness and system of the establishment...it fills the entire floor of a large office building."[35]

To the right of the reception room was the office, containing "huge volumes" of case records from the early years and pigeon-holes filled with records filed in envelopes, Miles' more recent system. The establishment also had a pharmacy and "consulting rooms" with "attending physicians." A drawing of the office shows a room carpeted with oriental rugs, with several men at desks along one wall, and facing them, two rows of female secretaries, to one of whom Miles seems to be dictating a letter.[36]

Miles and his family lived at the fashionable Chicago Beach Hotel. His son Charles and daughters, Marian and Electa, were now of marriageable age. In June, 1900, Electa was married to Robert Cleveland of Erie, Pennsylvania in a ceremony at the hotel. A. R. and A. H. Beardsley were among the Elkhart guests; Electa's finery included "white nun's veiling, with rare lace, a Gainsborough hat and diamond jewels." Two years later, Marian married John H. Collins of Elkhart, secretary of the Buescher Band Instrument Co. and a nephew of A. H. Beardsley.[37]

The Grand Dispensary and the Miles Observatory

The Miles' final return to Elkhart came between 1900 and 1902. In September 1900, Miles purchased the substantial home of Eber

Darling on the southwest corner of Fourth and Franklin Streets. It appears that the family moved in sometime the following year, with Miles commuting to Chicago and boarding at 325 Michigan Avenue.[38]

On January 18, 1902, the *Review* reported that the Dr. Franklin Miles Medical Association, "having outgrown its big headquarters in Chicago," would be moving to rooms on the second and third floors of Elkhart's spacious Bucklen Opera House on South Main Street. In March, "nearly 300 applicants for positions," mostly aspiring typists and stenographers, lined up at the Opera House for interviews, even though Miles stated that "he will bring fifteen experienced employees from Chicago and will probably employ nineteen in this city." A small office was kept in Chicago. It took four railroad cars, a week later, to move Miles' office furniture, equipment, records and medical supplies to Elkhart.[39]

The Grand Dispensary, which was incorporated under that name in November, 1904 with a capital stock of $50,000, now enjoyed its most prosperous years. Between the move to Elkhart and incorporation, business was reported to have doubled. The large daily correspondence kept some twenty typists and stenographers busy in what seems to have now become exclusively a mail operation. According to state statistics, employment peaked in 1906, with a total of forty-five employees, twelve men and thirty-three women. (The medical company, by contrast, employed 110.)[40]

Miles was a considerate "boss." Soon after the Grand Dispensary's establishment in the Bucklen Opera House, he fitted up a reading room/club room for his employees. That summer, the Miles hosted the "clerical and prescription force" and their families at a picnic in Elkhart's Island Park. And in September, 1903, Miles announced the trial of a profit-sharing plan for his department heads.[41]

A Dispensary pamphlet restated his opinions concerning the responsibilities physicians owed to their patients. In his 1905 booklet, *Golden Rules of Health, Deduced from the Lives of Many Famous Men Who Have Attained Ripe Old Age,* he insisted that a doctor's first duty was to teach his patients to live well.[42] He enumerated his "Golden Rules for the Sick," described "What to Eat and Drink" (and what not to), and listed ways "Patients can often assist their Physician in effecting a Cure."

In "Rules for Prolonging Life," he stressed avoidance of disease, sufficient exercise, proper diet (especially, not overeating), proper clothing, rest, healthful surroundings, avoidance of worry, and skilled medical treatment. The Grand Dispensary and Sanitarium, which by now had treated nearly 100,000 cases, could provide that treatment.[43]

Miles continued his close association with the Dr. Miles Medical Company, though still limiting his involvement in its operations. No letters or directives survive indicating that the Miles Weather Observatory was Dr. Miles' idea, but it seems extremely likely in view of his love of scientific observation.[44] Establishment of an accurate "weather station" at the Franklin Street plant to serve the Elkhart area lent authenticity to the new *Miles U. S. Weather Almanac and Handbook of Valuable Information.* The two developed in tandem.

In July, 1902, the *Review* reported that a structure twelve by twelve feet, and sixty feet high, was being erected on the roof of the Dr. Miles Medical Company. C. B. Linney, assistant observer of the Chicago weather bureau, came to oversee the installation and testing of meteorological instruments.

By October, multicolored "weather flags" were in place to give frequent forecasts to the community. They foretold fair or stormy weather and changes in temperature. Statistics also were compiled and furnished to the newspapers on temperature, rainfall, sunshine and cloudiness. Never before had Elkhart residents had such a service available to them.[45]

A U.S. Weather Bureau official said, "At the present time there is but one other private observatory in the United States which in completeness and excellence of equipment approaches that which you have installed...the famous Blue Hill observatory at Blue Hill, Mass."[46]

The *Almanac*, first issued in February 1902 with a run of 6,500,000 copies, portrayed on its cover some of the colorful flags and devices used at the company's and other weather observatories. The *Almanac* was to prove a most successful advertising vehicle for forty years.[47]

In early issues, Dr. Miles' influence seems apparent in short articles on health wedged between weather information, information for the household and farm, general-interest articles, and testimonials. One such health article described the "battleground" of the nervous system; another explained the cause and progress of "La Grippe." A third offered to send free advice and a symptom blank to readers who "do not understand your trouble, or are not getting the results you ought to get from the treatment you are taking." Presumably these inquiries were passed on to the Grand Dispensary.[48]

There was now, understandably, some confusion in the minds of distant customers between the Dr. Miles Medical Company and the Grand Dispensary, both located in Elkhart. Clerks spent time shuffling correspondence labeled "Dr. Miles" back and forth. Eventually, company literature and advertising began to carry the name "Miles Medical Co." without the "Dr.," and even on occasion to say, "Do not address, Dr. Miles."[49]

Another company project in which Miles may have had a hand was the "Dr. Miles' Plan," an elaborate, expensive, aggressive system instituted by the company in 1903 to keep a tighter grip on the sales practices of the wholesalers and retailers who handled Miles Medical Company products, and thus increase profits.

Under the "Plan," every bottle and box that left the company was individually numbered and tracked all the way to its final sale. Every retailer had to sign a contract agreeing to sell each Miles Medical Company product at a designated price, and to stamp his name on each item sold. The company reserved a "refusal to sell" to customers who would not honor its pricing policies in retailing products.[50]

In 1904, the company announced the plan's success in "98 per cent of the towns in the United States." According to a later source, Miles contributed substantially from his own funds toward this system.[51]

Though the company was still prospering, with a new four-story addition in 1903-04, there were clouds on the horizon. Public suspicion of the secret formulations of proprietary medicine makers was growing, thanks to the publication of "exposés" in *Collier's* and other popular magazines. The company kept away from launching new products. Its contract marketing system, too, was to run into strong opposition.

For now, Franklin Miles took some time simply to enjoy the life of a successful businessman. He went to considerable expense to remodel his new home on West Franklin Street and to acquire more land for lawn on the west side. He hired a gardener to care for the flowers. Elizabeth, who had a flair for interior decorating, helped her husband furnish the spacious two-story house. Among their most treasured possessions was a circular bronze chandelier with hanging prisms which had once hung at Williamsburg.[52]

In addition, Miles built a ten-room summer cottage for his family at Christiana Lake, which he christened "The Wigwam." It occupied the highest point near the lake, with a view of nearby Juno and Eagle lakes.[53]

Social functions were absorbing. In October, 1902, Elizabeth's niece, Margie State, married Edward Bartley in "the most elaborate wedding that ever took place in this city," followed by a reception at the Miles house on Franklin Street. In December 1902, the Roys hosted a debut party at the Century Club for Miss Julia Howland, with 200 local and out-of-town guests.[54]

In addition to the facilities of the Century Club on Main Street, of which Miles was elected president in 1904, there was the new Kenwood Country Club. (Miles also had helped found the Kenwood Club of Chicago in 1902-03.) Located beside the St. Joseph River on East Jackson Boulevard, the country club offered golfing, boating, and meals.

Here the men of Elkhart society, *en masse,* took up golf. At its opening tournament in 1904, president A. H. Beardsley personally entertained sixty men, many of whom were trying golf for the first time. Miles served on the club's board along with his son, Charles Franklin, now nearly thirty, a new director of the medical company and his father's assistant at The Grand Dispensary. Franklin Miles was so taken with golf that he planned a six weeks' golfing trip to California with the A.

H. Beardsleys in the spring of 1904.[55]

Another important part of his leisure was his "Thomas gasoline touring car" which arrived in July, 1903. A year later he had bought a Baker electric auto for Elizabeth. Miles and other auto owners organized an Elkhart Auto Club, which held its first banquet at the Kenwood Country Club in September, 1905.[56]

Family members emphasize that though Miles had become a wealthy and influential man, owned considerable property, and had earned ample leisure, he was free of the personal egotism and pretensions that can go with such wealth and influence.

Sickness and death, however, also struck Miles and his family in this period. Sometime during these years, Elizabeth lost a second child at birth, a son. And on September 24, 1904, the *Review* reported that while traveling Miles had become acutely ill, just after his arrival in Chicago, with inflammation of the bowels, a fever of 104 degrees, and for a time, a lapse of consciousness. He was, however, slowly, steadily improving at his hotel room in the Palmer House, tended by Mrs. Miles and a trained nurse.

Some days earlier, in Elkhart, their daughter Frances also had become ill; and on September 29, after an illness of some twenty days, she died, of malaria, according to her official record of death. It is not known if the two infections were connected.[57]

Soon there came a happier family event: the wedding of Charles Franklin Miles and Rachel Beardsley, sister of Andrew H. Beardsley, on October 20, 1904. It was a simple gathering at the home of Rachel's parents, the Solomon Lehman Beardsleys, and "all effort at elaborate pretension was eschewed," except for a wedding "bower" of autumn leaves illuminated by small electric lights. Now two of the medical company's leading families were even more closely linked, boding well for the future affairs of the company.[58]

Miles was beginning to groom Charles to take over management of the Grand Dispensary, for his mind was turning toward retirement. Perhaps with the idea of trying farming in his retirement years, he bought the Adamsville, Michigan farm of Frank Anselme, "the Quaker

Doctor," in the fall of 1905.[59]

He and Elizabeth had other absorbing interests as well: most importantly, the arrival of their first grandchildren, including Franklin Beardsley Miles and John Hyde Collins, Jr. There were family drives in a new White Steamer automobile.[60] Miles was a Master Mason, and Elizabeth an enthusiastic member of the Fifteen Circle Association, a literary club that was studying such topics as "Our Island World" and "Psychic Phenomena."[61]

And then there was Florida. Miles had clearly fallen in love with it. In January, 1905, he wrote Roys from Miami, saying that despite some unusually cool weather (he had, in fact, witnessed a damaging Florida citrus "freeze"), their trip had had a "remarkably beneficial effect upon our health." He reported jubilantly that one day, in just two and a half hours, he and Elizabeth had caught over 500 pounds of fish.[62]

Dr. Miles with children, Electa, Marian, and Charles Franklin, about 1893.

Classic Dr. Miles' Nervine bottle and packaging.

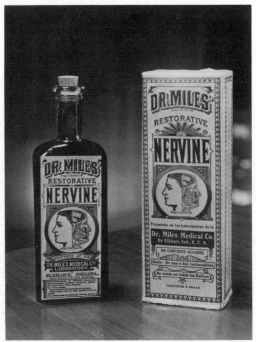

Advertising copy for direction, Dr. Miles' Anti-Pain Pills, ca. 1900, showing Dr. Miles' corrections.

Nerve and Liver Pills. Take as soon as headache begins for best results. A dose or two when symptoms first appear will usually prevent an attack. See full directions on last page.

Nervous Headache–Take Dr. Miles' Anti-Pain Pills
   The more common varieties of headache are nervous, ocular, sick, bilious, neuralgic, anaemic, plethoric and catarrhal. As all these varieties of pain are removed by the use of Anti-Pain Pills, Dr. Miles has been lead to regard them as due to irritation of the nerve centers.
   Directions: For adults, take an Anti-Pain Pill immediately. It may be swallowed whole, dissolved in water or chewed and swallowed. If the pain is not relieved in twenty minutes, take another. In bad cases two may be taken at first dose, and if not relieved in an hour another may be taken, and hourly thereafter, if needed, until six are used. It is not advisable to take more than six in 24 hours. (Many persons, however, take these pills in more frequent doses with beneficial results.) When the bowels are constipated, Dr. Miles' Nerve and Liver Pills should be taken. In chronic or frequent headaches, Dr. Miles' Nervine should also be used for a time.
Neuralgic Pains–Take Dr. Miles' Anti-Pain Pills.
   There is certainly no more effectual remedy for neuralgic pain than Dr. Miles' Anti-Pain Pills. If debilitated also take Dr. Miles' Restorative Tonic.
      See full directions on last page.

Ocular Headache–Take Dr. Miles' Anti-Pain Pills.
   For this form of headache Dr. Miles' Anti-Pain Pills are especially recommended, as they seldom fail to remove the pain. As they are not intended to remove the eye strain, subsequent attacks are likely to occur, and in such cases the constant wearing of proper spectacles will be found very beneficial.
   Directions: For adults; on the first indications of headache take an Anti-Pain Pill, and the attack will be prevented. Persons who usually experience disagreeable effects from attending church, theatres, should take a pill before going. See full directions on last page.
Rheumatic Pains–Take Dr. Miles' Anti-Pain Pills.
   They are very beneficial in the pains of rheumatism, and in many cases assist in the cure. See directions on last page. Dr. Miles' Restorative Nervine should also be taken as directed for rheumatism.
Backache, Lumbago–
Take Dr. Miles' Anti-Pain Pills.
These common ailments are readily relieved with Dr. Miles' Anti-Pain Pills.

Ocular Headache–Take Dr. Miles' Anti-Pain Pills.
   Ocular headaches are very common, being those caused by reading, sewing, attending church, theatres, riding, looking intently, etc. For this form of headache Dr. Miles' Anti-Pain Pills are especially recommended, as they seldom fail to remove the pain.
   Directions: For adults; on the first indications of headache take an Anti-Pain Pill, and the attack will be prevented. See full directions on last page.
Rheumatic Pains–Take Dr. Miles' Anti-Pain Pills.
   They are very beneficial in the pains of rheumatism, and in many cases assist in the cure. See directions on last page. Dr. Miles' Restorative Nervine should also be taken as directed for rheumatism.
Backache, Lumbago–
Take Dr. Miles' Anti-Pain Pills.
These common ailments are readily relieved with Dr. Miles' Anti-Pain Pills.

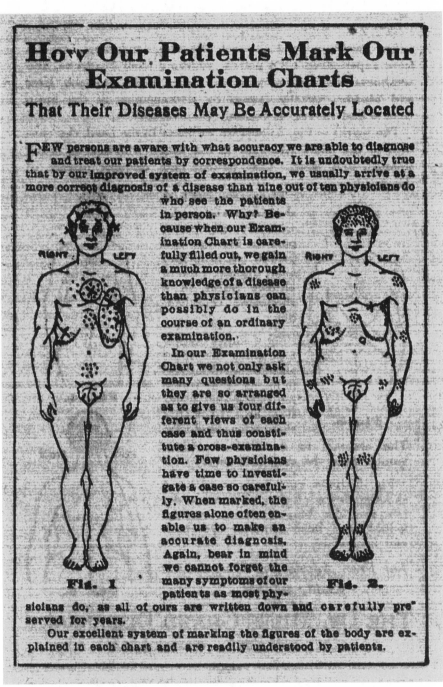

How Our Patients Mark Our Examination Charts

That Their Diseases May Be Accurately Located

FEW persons are aware with what accuracy we are able to diagnose and treat our patients by correspondence. It is undoubtedly true that by our improved system of examination, we usually arrive at a more correct diagnosis of a disease than nine out of ten physicians do who see the patients in person. Why? Because when our Examination Chart is carefully filled out, we gain a much more thorough knowledge of a disease than physicians can possibly do in the course of an ordinary examination.

In our Examination Chart we not only ask many questions but they are so arranged as to give us four different views of each case and thus constitute a cross-examination. Few physicians have time to investigate a case so carefully. When marked, the figures alone often enable us to make an accurate diagnosis. Again, bear in mind we cannot forget the many symptoms of our patients as most physicians do, as all of ours are written down and carefully preserved for years.

Our excellent system of marking the figures of the body are explained in each chart and are readily understood by patients.

Fig. 1

Fig. 2

Courtesy Miles Archives.

Portion of the Dr. Miles Grand Dispensary's self-examination chart.

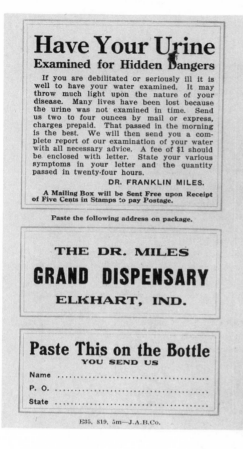

Have Your Urine
Examined for Hidden Dangers

If you are debilitated or seriously ill it is well to have your water examined. It may throw much light upon the nature of your disease. Many lives have been lost because the urine was not examined in time. Send us two to four ounces by mail or express, charges prepaid. That passed in the morning is the best. We will then send you a complete report of our examination of your water with all necessary advice. A fee of $1 should be enclosed with letter. State your various symptoms in your letter and the quantity passed in twenty-four hours.

DR. FRANKLIN MILES.

A Mailing Box will be Sent Free upon Receipt of Five Cents in Stamps to pay Postage.

Paste the following address on package.

THE DR. MILES
GRAND DISPENSARY
ELKHART, IND.

Paste This on the Bottle
YOU SEND US

Name ....
P. O. ....
State ....

E35, 819, 5m—J.A.B.Co.

HIDDEN DANGERS

Why Your Urine Should Be Examined.

EVERYBODY whether sick or well, should occasionally have his urine examined by a chemist, as such an examination will throw a certain and important light upon the condition of the system. Disease of the kidneys, or other parts of the body, can often be detected in this manner, long before it would otherwise be known to exist. Persons often have Bright's Disease, or Sugar Diabetes, for weeks or months before it is suspected.

An examination of the urine is therefore advisable in all chronic or lingering diseases, and absolutely necessary to the successful treatment of many serious cases.

Aware of this important aid in recognizing disease, Dr. Miles has established and equipped a special Laboratory in the Dispensary. This department of The Grand Dispensary is supplied with appliances and instruments of precision for making delicate tests of the different fluids and tissues of the body. Every sample of urine is carefully analyzed and examined by our chemist.

It is a deplorable fact that the majority of physicians neglect this important branch of advanced medical science, either from ignorance, carelessness, lack of skill or their inability to procure the costly instruments needed for making accurate examinations.

A Poisonous Fluid.

The urine is a fluid containing the waste and poisonous products of the body which are taken by the blood from the various parts of the system, and should be carried off by means of the kidneys. Every change occuring in the blood, nerves and organs of the

Articles from flyer, Dr. Miles Grand Dispensary.

Dr. Franklin L. Miles, ca. 1905.

6
Florida, 1906-1929

"Miles of River Frontage"

Fort Myers was still just a little town in the midst of much wild country when Franklin Miles and Cyrus Roys and their wives were guests at its Royal Palm Hotel in February, 1906. Drawn by the huge tarpon, plentiful trout, redfish, snapper, and many other varieties of fish, wealthy sportsmen had been making this area of south Florida's Gulf coast, with its islands and its wide river, the Caloosahatchee, a winter vacation spot for two decades.

Though Fort Myers had developed as a cattle trading center, the land around it remained mostly undeveloped. More recently, however, Lee County's tropical climate had begun to attract citrus growing on a large scale, and the extension of rail service in 1904 opened numerous possibilities for growth.

Vacationers were often enticed to permanent winter settlement. They joined the "older" families in building fine homes on First Street facing the Caloosahatchee, and contributing to town life. Fort Myers' most famous winter resident was Thomas Edison, whose estate was an arboretum of tropical plants from all over the world.[1]

By this time, sixty-year-old Dr. Franklin Miles could most definitely be characterized as wealthy. His earnings from the medical company, the dispensary, and Elkhart real estate made him a potential large investor in Fort Myers' future. And he was much in need of a winter home, according to several accounts. Whether it was recurring bouts of pneumonia, bronchitis, or other lung afflictions, his doctors strongly advised him to avoid northern winters.

In mid-March, 1906, Miles stopped a *Fort Myers Press* reporter and told him that they "had the making of a beautiful and popular winter resort here, but that the town must keep up the cows, and give the palms and other tropical trees a chance to grow on our streets." He added that the trees would attract visitors to Fort Myers.[2]

The following year, Thomas Edison would donate hundreds of royal palms to line the boulevards; and a livestock containment ordinance would be enacted in 1908. It is not known if Miles had a part in bringing these things about, but at any rate, he did not wait for these improvements. In September, 1906, he purchased Walter Langford's large, attractive white frame house on First Street. There were sixteen rooms, a big screened porch, and an elegant staircase.[3]

For a short time during this period, Miles reportedly "retired," spending most of his hours fishing, relaxing, and socializing. But it was not long until his health was restored and new projects gripped his imagination and inspired all-out efforts.

His new interest was Florida land. Thousands of acres were available all around him, at low prices, and he saw possibilities of the land's development both as real estate and for agriculture. In the spring of 1907, after their first winter in the Fort Myers house, Miles undertook two major projects. One was to go into partnership with Frank A. Lane, a land developer and citrus grower, to develop a 100-acre citrus farm at Olga northeast of Fort Myers.

The second was to purchase some 2,000 acres along the Caloosahatchee a few miles south of Fort Myers in what is known as the Iona district. Some was for his own use, some to resell to prospective settlers. A tempting notice in the *Press* stated, "The property embraces miles of river frontage, much of it being located near the famous tarpon-fishing grounds, and all varieties of soil are represented, with many beautiful building sites, and unlimited possibilities for growing oranges, grapefruit and all tropical and semi-tropical fruits, and vegetables."[4]

Miles was entranced by the beauty of the river, a wide tidal stream bringing in currents from the Gulf twice a day. He prophetically believed that the area would someday draw residents and tourists by the millions. As for agriculture, the Iona district was almost sure to avoid the devastating effects of cold winter weather which he had noted on his Florida trip in 1905, for the district was not only the most frost-free in Lee County, but possibly in the entire continental United States.[5]

Iona already had many groves of oranges, grapefruit and limes.

Truck farming (vegetable growing), however, had been largely confined to nearby Captiva and Sanibel Islands.[6] Miles' venturesomeness lay in his desire to experiment with truck farming in Iona on a large scale, and make it viable for others as well. To do so required money, scientific investigation and experiment, involvement in politics, and educational effort. It was, in short, a project to engage all his abilities for some fifteen years. In many ways, these would be his happiest years.

Poinsettia Place

Franklin and Elizabeth Miles completed their settlement in Florida in the winter of 1908-09, when they moved into their "country" home, which they called the Shell House, on the bank of the river near the northwest corner of the new Iona property. The Shell House, so named because a gray finish of solid oyster shell coated its 18-inch-thick concrete walls, was an old house, built shortly after the Civil War, reputedly by a Confederate officer.

Abandoned soon after it was built, it had been used as a shelter by traveling cattlemen, and had the reputation of being haunted after a murder took place there. Miles, who had first admired the house on fishing trips, had it repaired, refurbished and enlarged. He installed a seawall and filled its acres of spacious grounds with a wide variety of tropical trees, shrubs and flowers, including bananas, mangoes, and coconut and royal palms.[7]

A regular routine was soon established: the Shell House in the winter, the Fort Myers house in the spring as it grew warmer and insects became bothersome, and a few weeks back in Elkhart in the summer and early fall, during Florida's least tolerable weather. The time spent in Elkhart grew less as years went by.[8]

In 1908 also, Franklin and Elizabeth Miles took an important step to fill the void left by the deaths of their two children. They informally adopted Louise, a three-year-old child who had been placed in a Florida orphanage.[9]

In the mid-1980s, when she was interviewed, Louise Miles Bass' memories of her early life with her adopted family were full and vibrant. The Shell House had a large, informal living room, a huge kitchen, a second-floor "sanctum" full of books and a first floor den (both for her father), and a widow's walk atop the red-shingled roof from which Louise had a fine view of the Caloosahatchee and the passing river craft that supplied Iona's main transportation.

Her father lost no time in developing and enlarging his land holdings. By November 1908, he had cleared 300 acres of his farm property, and the same month sold parcels to two local farmers. Over the next few years his Iona property grew until it stretched nearly eleven miles along the river, and over two miles inland at some spots. He also purchased properties across the river on Cape Coral, at various points upriver, and on Pine, Captiva and Estero Islands—many thousands of acres in all.[10]

He became known as a wise, cautious and conscientious developer, never reselling a parcel of land "until he knew what it was good for and could advise the purchaser in its use."[11]

In just one year, meanwhile, the Miles-Lane citrus farm at Olga, which they called Palm Grove, grew from 1,000 to 4,000 trees. Lane managed the thriving grove. In May 1908, a visitor from the *Press* marvelled at "one of the most prolific grapefruit and orange groves we have seen in many a day," with mature trees that seemed to have "as many as five boxes of fruit on them," and younger trees unaffected by a spring drought. Interspersed among the groves were acres of watermelons and tomatoes. An irrigation system, "equipped with the latest machinery," pumped water to the roots.[12]

By the spring of 1909, Miles was beginning to experiment with truck farming on his Iona farm, which he had named "Poinsettia Place." So many problems faced him that he was at first branded an eccentric by the locals. An earlier resident, a Dr. Harris of Key West, had abandoned efforts to cultivate about seventeen acres of the property. Miles later wrote, "All the old settlers said that the soil could not be made to pay taxes. It would only raise a disturbance."[13]

Not only was extensive irrigation needed in the dry season, but the rainy season dumped too much water on the land. Even more importantly, the soil was deficient in nutrients for vegetable growing, and local farmers lacked reliable knowledge of how to improve it. There were destructive insects unknown to northern climates. And on top of everything, the property was very isolated; there was no way through to Fort Myers, with its supplies and rail connections, except by water.[14]

Dissatisfied with several unsuccessful efforts by hired farm managers, on the advice of U. S. Department of Agriculture officials Miles personally studied and attacked his unique problems. He consulted experts in regard to every aspect of agriculture in the south Florida climate. In 1909-10, for example, he brought potato growers from Oklahoma to superintend the cultivation of his pioneering Irish potato crop, which spanned thirty-seven acres north of the Shell House.[15]

To determine what fertilizers to use and how to combat insect pests, Miles corresponded through the Department of Agriculture with farmers in similar climates as far away as China and Korea. As the farm developed, he built a small office-laboratory. Louise Bass recalled that it was stocked with jars full of insects, soil samples, books on tropical agriculture, and equipment to test soils, temperature and moisture.[16] He conducted what one source referred to as "a private agricultural station."[17]

Miles learned to enrich the soil by applying various combinations of marl, lime, rotten shell and ground phosphate rock. He learned to prepare "inoculated compost" whose virtues he extolled above those of chemical fertilizers.[18] Irrigation and drainage were taken care of by an elaborate grid of ditches connecting to Artesian wells. His first well was described by a reporter as having "a pressure that is fully able to throw water over his large two-story residence."[19]

To offset the farm's isolation, Miles developed a self-sufficient settlement containing over sixty buildings. In addition to the family home and cottages, there were cottages for forty farm employees and their families, barns, a sawmill, a blacksmith shop, a machine shop, a packing shed, and even a store, school and church.[20]

A 700-foot-long wagon wharf was built for effective connection with the river boats. Miles had boats of his own as well, including the launch "Chipmunk." Shipping on the Caloosahatchee was not totally reliable. It was improved, however, in 1910 when a Federal project straightened and deepened the river.[21]

While developing his farm, Miles also worked toward breaking its isolation. He took an active part in the drive to get a road constructed from Fort Myers through his farm to Punta Rassa on the south. McGregor Boulevard would be completed in 1915.[22]

Florida, Louise Bass remembered, was "hard on people." Her mother, especially, was frightened by the wild countryside and its hidden dangers: omnipresent snakes, an occasional glimpse of panthers and wildcats, biting insects, the threat of fires in the dry season.

Neither Franklin nor Elizabeth was in perfect health (Elizabeth had a heart condition), and no medical care, other than Franklin's own, was available. Franklin, and Louise as she grew older, became Elizabeth's protectors. Miles, by contrast, seemed to draw strength from his vigorous outdoor life. Louise Bass remembered his strong, striding "athlete's" walk as he toured the farm each day.[23]

To balance the demanding life of the farm, the social and civic activities of Fort Myers were important to them both. They must often have boated upstream to their house in town during the winter months. The Royal Palm Hotel was full of guests, including Cyrus and Katherine Roys, who continued their visits year after year.

Parties were frequent. At one costume ball, described in the *Press* as a "Book Party," each guest appeared as "some famous novel." The Miles, tightly clasping each other, portrayed *To Have and to Hold*. In 1909, Miles and Roys helped organized the Caloosahatchee Fishing and Hunting Club to promote greater social interaction between permanent residents and vacationers, and to encourage and regulate local fishing and hunting.[24]

Elizabeth Miles, as always, enjoyed entertaining, and gave parties for friends and visiting family at the First Street house. Louise Bass recalls that the Edisons were among her parents' good friends. On at least one occasion, however, the great inventor was aloof toward Louise.

Her father told her it was because of his deafness. They visited back and forth, and Edison furnished Miles with roots and cuttings for his gardens.[25]

Civic activities were important, too. These were years of growing prosperity and downtown building and improvements in Fort Myers. Miles took part in funding a seawall and buildup of land along First Street.[26]

The yearly trips to Elkhart, also important in their routine, were dictated more by the need to escape the Florida heat and "rainy season," and to see Elkhart friends, than by company demands. The Beardsleys were capably managing the company in these years, achieving not only survival but increased sales with the company's basically good products, in the face of scathing and widespread attacks on the patent medicine industry, and a historic judgement against the "vertical price-fixing" practices of the "Miles Plan" by the U. S. Supreme Court.

The Beardsleys, who were extremely active in the American Proprietary Association and influential in both state and national politics, helped produce food and drug legislation that not only benefited their own company, but manufacturers in general. Miles made large financial contributions toward these efforts; no doubt his advice was solicited as well.[27]

In 1911, annual meetings of the company, now an Indiana co-partnership, were changed from December to summer so that Miles could attend. The next year, however, Miles began the process of transferring his stock to other family members.[28] All three of his adult children were well settled in Elkhart; by 1915 Charles and Rachel Beardsley Miles owned the Franklin Street house. Charles, now in total charge of the Grand Dispensary, and also a vice president of the medical company, frequently sought his father's advice.

The Grand Dispensary, unlike the medical company, was beginning to decline as the popularity of its types of services lessened.[29] One Dispensary pamphlet bearing signs of Miles's authorship survives from this period. *Golden Rules for Recovering Health and Prolonging Life*

(1911) reprinted much of the advice in the earlier *Golden Rules*. But there was a new emphasis on the power of the mind over disease, and substitution of the term "Psychic Force" for "Nerve Force." "Psychic Force," or "Animal Electricity," was conducted not only by the nerves, but by the air, from one mind to another.

Psychic force was generated not only by the brain, but also by a second "brain," whose location was not specified. It appears that by the age of sixty-five, life had revived or strengthened Miles' long-held interest in psychic phenomena. (It would be interesting to know if parallels could be found in recent research on mind-body interaction and chemical receptors outside the brain.)[30]

Miles had other business interests in Elkhart. For example, he was listed as president of the board of the Citizens Trust Company, established in 1910. No doubt he was a substantial stockholder as well. The board of this new bank, which offered full banking services, also included two of his old medical colleagues. It was located at Main and Marion streets.[31]

Family gatherings were an important part of the annual summer trips. Descendants remembered trips to New England to see the Hamlin relatives. Miles "commissioned" the writing of a genealogy by his cousin, Lucretia Belle Hamlin. Much time was spent also at Christiana Lake, where in addition to his cottage Miles built the Christiana Lake Tavern.

Miles built this large, brown-shingled lodge as a hotel in 1910. It had some fifty guest rooms; nearby were several small cottages and outbuildings. After a few years, he discontinued its operation as a hotel but continued to rent the cottages, and utilized the lodge for family and social gatherings. Miles sold the Christiana Lake Tavern and his other Michigan property in 1916, when the yearly trips to Elkhart were becoming shorter.[32]

Courtesy Miles Archives.

The ever-popular Miles Almanac.

Courtesy Hartzler-Gutermuth-Inman Funeral Home.

The Miles home at 403 W. Franklin, Elkhart, purchased in 1900.

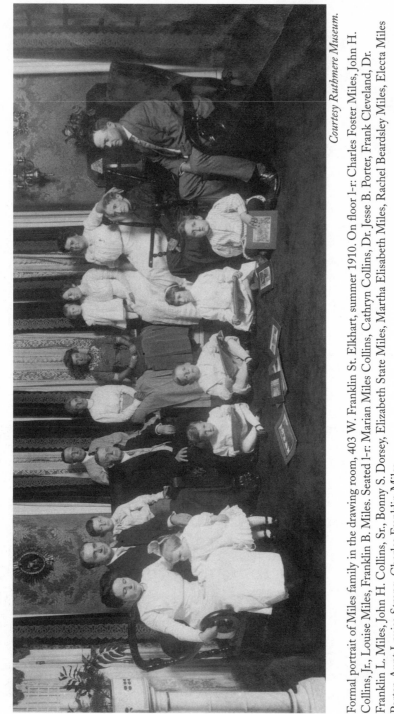

Formal portrait of Miles family in the drawing room, 403 W. Franklin St. Elkhart, summer 1910. On floor l-r: Charles Foster Miles, John H. Collins, Jr., Louise Miles, Franklin B. Miles. Seated l-r: Marian Miles Collins, Cathryn Collins, Dr. Jesse B. Porter, Frank Cleveland, Dr. Franklin L. Miles, John H. Collins, Sr., Bonny S. Dorsey, Elizabeth State Miles, Martha Elisabeth Miles, Rachel Beardsley Miles, Electa Miles Porter, Aunt Louisa Strong, Charles Franklin Miles.

Advertisement from *Elkhart Truth*, Progress Number, 1924.

The Patriarch

The farm at Iona truly blossomed in the years just before, during and after World War I, and farm and family life in the Shell House and its surrounding cottages was memorable.[33]

Every fall the Shell House began to fill with additional family as Miles' three grown children and their families, Elizabeth's mother Theresa State, Franklin's uncle Lorenzo Miles, and other relatives came for visits of varying length. Some became permanent winter residents, with their own cottages on the grounds.

Louise Bass remembered wonderful times with the Miles grandchildren, some of whom were her own age, and also adventurous escapades in the still-wild country, roaming the fields alone on horseback, carrying a rifle her father trained her very early to use, always on the lookout for poisonous snakes.[34]

The children spent many hours with the farm employees, including Charles Tierney, the chauffeur-boat pilot-mechanic, who took the children "fire-fishing" at night. They speared bountiful quantities of fish, which they shared with the farm hands. At Christmas, Elizabeth gave parties for the employees' children.

Dr. Miles, with Louise as his assistant, supplied routine medical services for the employees, including dosing for malaria and treating cuts and accidents. Elizabeth and Louise also drove from cottage to cottage, making sure the workers' families were properly refrigerating their milk. Boats brought groceries every few days, and mail daily.[35]

Every day the extended Miles family, including children, grandchildren and two orphaned cousins from Canada the Miles had taken under their wing, assembled for lunch and dinner in the large Shell House dining room. Two ample tables seated sixteen adults, nine children, and a governess. There were after-dinner musicales, charades for the children, and nightly poker games for the adults.[36]

At other times, Elizabeth would gather all the children in the "den" to tell them delightful stories; or Franklin would assemble them for lectures which the grandchildren remembered were "far over their heads." He chose topics such as "Do you want to be a work horse or a race horse?", "Marry for intelligence," and "Marry tall people."[37]

Miles taught his children and grandchildren to argue their opinions, but never to fight, believing that families should settle their differences reasonably. He exemplified and taught good manners, reprimanded the children for criticizing and for cruel pranks, supervised their dietary habits, and emphasized physical fitness. They had to learn to swim, in the pool he built for the purpose, to box (lessons were given by Miles himself), and to ride. In the mornings, there were tutored school lessons.[38]

He taught courage, advising Louise never to show fear or doubt; and never to "turn your back on your troubles." He taught her to treasure beauty, telling her one evening to keep the extraordinary colors of a Florida sunset in her heart.

He taught resilience, portraying life as a series of falls from which one must right oneself and move on. In one often-repeated anecdote, he pointed to a tree that had survived a recent hurricane by being able to "bend to the storm." He taught prudence, advising that one's words and actions were like pebbles whose ripples could reach others in unknown ways.[39] (There is evidence that a number of his own statements and actions were designed to protect, rather than to reveal.)

He taught that no religion had a monopoly on sanctity, that all held basically the same beliefs and ethical values. And according to his daughter, he compared the universal life force to electricity which is present even when a light bulb is broken and cannot receive it.[40]

Miles also taught the youngsters to play poker for small stakes. He let them examine his shell collections. And he always had answers for their questions, no matter how obscure, even if it meant a trip upstairs to consult the books in his "sanctum." Louise Bass remembers both her parents as great readers, staying up past midnight with their books—Franklin reading of "darkest Africa" or other exotic places, or exploring the many worlds of religion, Elizabeth preferring murder mysteries.[41]

Louise Bass remembers that it was a happy marriage, with much warm affection in evidence. Bass draws a vivid picture of her father in these later years. Tanned and neatly dressed, usually wearing his glasses and chomping on a cigar, he worked in his first floor den, addressing problems related to the farm, his Fort Myers holdings and financial affairs, and the Elkhart businesses, all in quick succession, from a messy desk no one dared touch.

His baritone voice could often be heard on the telephone, and he handled employees and other visitors with a gentle air of authority (Chesterfield would have called it *"suaviter in modo, fortiter in re"*) that "quieted people down" if they were distressed or excited. His expensive toupee was a matter of fascination to the children, and had a way of slipping off or being askew on his head that caused much merriment. He was troubled with a chronic cough, the result of his lung problems. Yet he walked over the entire farm every day.[42]

Dr. Miles' economic interests were prospering. In 1913 he formed a corporation, the Franklin Miles Association, to take ownership of the land on behalf of the family and to handle mortgages, investments in stocks and bonds, and borrowing and loaning of funds. A description of the properties turned over by the family to the corporation in 1915 takes up eight pages in the Lee County Recorder's records. Their holdings included the Fishermen's Lodge hotel on Captiva Island, which Miles had purchased after it was severely damaged by a storm in 1910.[43]

The Miles family, including the three grown children and their spouses, now approaching middle age, were contributing to the civic and philanthropic life of Fort Myers. Elizabeth's pride was the Elizabeth Benevolent Society, which furnished linens for the new Fort Myers hospital established in 1915.

Electa Miles' second husband, Dr. Jesse B. Porter, an eye, ear, nose and throat specialist from Elkhart, served on the Fort Myers city council and board of trade. And Electa was hostess to the wife of Vice President Marshall during Mrs. Marshall's visit to Fort Myers in 1914. Women of the Miles family were active in Red Cross work during World War I, and in other local charities.[44]

It was a good time to be involved in truck farming. Iona farmers were rapidly increasing their acreage, and growing a diversity of commercial crops. In the fall of 1917, the *Press* reported that in four or five years the quantity of vegetables shipped by rail from Fort Myers had risen from one to 300 carloads a year.[45]

Though his largest acreage was still in Irish potatoes, Miles had added other crops, including green peppers, cabbage, eggplants, tomatoes, mangoes, and melons. He investigated commercial sugar cane growing briefly, but decided after a trip to Cuba that it would be uneconomical to compete with Cuban growers. He did plant some sugar cane, and built a syrup mill on the farm to process cane for the farm's use.[46]

The growth of Iona's truck crops was greatly stimulated by the shortages and rising prices of World War I. Miles increased his overall acreage in potatoes and vegetables, and branched out into rice and avocados. In October, 1917, he also had six tenants, and with Lane's death he now totally owned the Olga citrus grove. To help make the larger crops possible in wartime, Louise Bass remembered that additional female field hands were hired at Poinsettia Place.[47]

Green peppers, especially, provided a bonanza for truck farmers around Fort Myers. Local papers reported a rapid rise in their production and value; Miles went from twenty to fifty acres of peppers between 1917 and 1919. It was not unusual for an acre of peppers to bring in over $1,000. Boosting this growth was the Fort Myers (Lee County) Truckers Association, organized by Miles and others in 1917. For several years there had been a citrus packing and joint marketing organization, but none for truck farmers.

By the fall of 1918 their new packing house was in operation, packing and shipping a carload of peppers daily under the Rainbow brand. Inside the plant, in a converted warehouse on Hendry Street in Fort Myers, special pepper sorting and grading equipment speeded up the work considerably.

The system was designed by Miles. Peppers were dumped from a hopper onto a conveyor belt. Women stood alongside, letting the larger peppers go on to be manually packed, sorting the smaller ones onto parallel running belts which deposited them into packing boxes. Two years later, further improvements were made, and the brand name was changed to Seven Stars.[48]

Miles also gained local fame for his cultivation of avocados. He experimented with several varieties, and in early 1919 produced what the *Press* called "a new, nice, meaty avocado with only 5% seed." His vegetables and fruits, as well as those of his neighbors, were exhibited and won prizes at fairs, including the Florida State Fair and the Kansas City International Exposition. Miles was now considered an authority on horticultural and agricultural matters. In 1917, for example, the *Press* noted his advice in regard to the dying royal palms on the outskirts of town: that the soil be fertilized to make it more like that of downtown Fort Myers.[49]

Transportation continued to be a concern to the people of south Florida. In November 1917, Governor Catts and his top officials visited Fort Myers and reported progress on plans to install locks on the Caloosahatchee "to preserve the uniformity of the waterway its entire length." They also promised, at a crowded mass meeting in the Lee County courthouse, to work for the completion of a cross-state waterway and roads. This project would mean resumption of drainage work through the Everglades suspended years before. During their visit, the officials toured Miles' 700-acre farm.[50]

New Challenges in the Last Years

We were getting a cottage ready for one of the relatives to come down...and the housekeeper was over there with us, and Mother was directing what she wanted done. All of a sudden she walked out on the porch and she said, "Well, look at the big black cloud coming up off the horizon. We had better get back to the house before it rains." I looked out and it was a clear blue sky. Not a cloud. So I said, "Miss Peal, you stay with Mother. I'm going to get Daddy." I ran just as fast as I could back to the house. By the time I got Daddy back there, she was blind.

(Memoirs of Louise Miles Bass, 1983)

A new care and concern had entered Franklin Miles' life. It had not come totally without warning; some time earlier, Louise had accompanied her mother to Chicago for surgery on her eyes, and that surgery had not been completely successful. Resolving to make the best of things, and with the help of Franklin, and all of her family, Elizabeth learned to cope with her loss of sight.

Some years later, Miles wrote A. H. Beardsley, "Lizzie has learned to write on the typewriter without being able to see the typewriter herself, about as well as the average typist. She does all her writing in an absolutely dark room." She also learned to read Braille. But the family kept a constant watch lest she either fall or overexert her heart.[51]

Another worry assailed Miles from a different direction. Local drainage projects designed to open more land to agriculture were being promoted in various parts of Florida, financed by special assessments. The Iona Drainage District project, organized in 1919, was fiercely opposed by Miles and his friends because of what they felt were illegal methods, such as including some Iona landowners in the project without their knowledge, inflated costs, and unscientific techniques (ditches that were too deep).

Miles forcefully argued his case in several newspaper articles, and in March 1921 "Miles et al." brought suit against the company. Construction stopped. Though a settlement was announced in January, 1922, modifications having been made in the plan to provide "satisfactory drainage" with a saving of taxpayers' money, the controversy was still on his mind nearly a year later, according to his letter to Hub Beardsley: "Have been exceedingly busy with farm, groves, drainage fight (single handed against a crowd of crooks) . . . the Drainage District will prove one of the worst failures in Southern Florida."[52]

Characteristically, despite his problems, Miles did not stop spinning off new projects and bringing them to full development. In 1921, the *Fort Myers Tropical News* announced that Miles had cleared 1,000 acres, not for his own use, but for rental to other farmers. If his project proved a success, he intended to rent thousands more. It also was announced that he would teach his tenants and other local farmers the principles of truck farming in the tropical environment, through a newly established "Truckers' School."

"Hundreds of thousands of acres of virgin land lie idle in Lee County," Miles told the *Tropical News*, "but just as soon as the farmers here learn to use the land, then the world will make a beaten path to Lee county and it will be a veritable garden of Eden." He reminded the reporter about American farmers of earlier years who had gone to Kansas and had come back "busted" because they did not learn new farming techniques for the new country.

The "Truckers' School" sessions, to be held weekly, would include lectures by Miles and other successful farmers, and the county agent, with time also for an "open forum or debating society." Louise Bass remembered that the classes were held in her father's office, and that he made available to the farmers his books on agriculture in tropical countries.[53]

Miles promoted his school and land rental program with a large, illustrated flyer titled on one side, *Dr. Miles Premium Farm* and on the other, *A Free Practical School for Truckers*. The brochure, successor to so many bold advertisements for his medicines, tempted potential settlers with praises of the Fort Myers landscape and climate, and description of the farm. He praised its plentiful irrigation, and fields pre-fertilized with "six to ten tons of lime or marl—a splendid plant food—and two or more tons of ground pebble phosphate rock to each acre."

There were photographs of Miles with Governor Catts and his delegation, Miles' winning displays at the 1919 Florida State Fair and Kansas City International Exposition, and farm scenes. There were excerpts from laudatory newspaper articles—much like the testimonials of old. Miles taught the truckers "how to test his soil" and "how to best prepare soil for seed beds and crops. How and when to fertilize, cultivate, irrigate, spray, pick, pack and ship and how to prepare homemade composts and other fertilizers thus saving considerable money; and also how to build up, rather than exhaust soils."

Another project Miles developed in these years was renovating and opening the Fishermen's Lodge on Captiva Island. Facing Pine Island sound, the rustic hotel accommodated fishermen during the January 1 to June 1 fishing season. Later advertised as "The Resort of

Roosevelt and Wanamaker," it offered rooms with running water and electricity, and boat rentals. In December, 1922, Miles was "painting, furnishing, papering, and generally refitting" it, and in early 1923, shortly after it opened, he wrote,

"There seems to be a good prospect of having to double the size of Fishermen's Lodge this fall . . . within twenty-seven days from the time it opened the Lodge was compelled to turn away customers for want of rooms and a month later its business was surprising everybody, including myself. We are taking in $150.00 a day on the average and have a . . . waiting list. We are also surprised at the fine quality of our patrons."[54]

Gradually, Miles began to spend less time on the farm than before. Elizabeth Miles had always felt the isolation of the farm (even with the new road, Fort Myers friends visited infrequently). Now, in her blindness, she felt that isolation much more keenly.

According to letters from A. H. Beardsley, Franklin Miles' health also began to deteriorate. At some point they began to live primarily in Fort Myers, with Miles driving the eight miles back and forth to the farm as needed. His trips, daily at first, gradually became less, until he finally stopped personally attending to the farm's operations.

Louise and her father helped make Elizabeth's life as safe and happy as possible. They tried not to leave her alone, and made sure that every feature of the First Street house, especially the living room, which became her "headquarters," was familiar. From this room, Elizabeth dispensed affection and help to her family and friends. Often, in the evenings, Louise read for hours to her mother, her favorite mysteries, with Miles listening.[55]

More and more, Fort Myers became their world. Miles kept busy. Though his farm operations declined, there were the Lodge and all his property interests to oversee. Miles was enthusiastic when a major real estate boom developed in Fort Myers upon the long-hoped-for completion of the cross-state highway known as the Tamiani Trail. He participated in the boom by building a $75,000 apartment house on McGregor Boulevard, completed in 1926. He also served as a director of the First National Bank of Fort Myers.[56]

In several letters, A. H. Beardsley warned him from Elkhart about the inevitable "bursting" of the Fort Myers boom. But Miles resolutely clung to his optimism about its permanence. "During the last fifty years," he wrote Beardsley, "the opinion of the northern people have been gradually changing regarding the desirability of living south and during this period, many northern people have become quite wealthy. It has been estimated that five or ten million of these people are thinking about going to Florida to prolong their lives and have a more agreeable winter season . . . until they have come, the boom will not 'peter' out."[57]

The boom of the 1920s did end in Fort Myers, however, partly as a result of one of the worst hurricanes in Florida history, which struck in September, 1926, wrecking buildings and doing millions of dollars in damage. It would take more years for Miles' predictions to be proven correct.[58]

Other sorrows and storms, however, were also buffeting the Miles' lives. Some years before there had come the death of his closest friend, Cyrus Roys, and of Elizabeth's mother, Theresa State. Then, in 1923, Marian's husband John H. Collins, died, and her son John Collins, Jr. died the next year. Probably in the fall or winter of 1925-26, the Shell House burned to the ground, with many of their treasured possessions. This loss was a great blow to Miles.[59]

The news from Elkhart was not encouraging. Though the company was holding its own and further enlarged its plant in 1924, criticism of both the company and the Grand Dispensary by the A.M.A. had been intensifying for some time. In 1921 some of Miles' preparations were condemned in the A.M.A.'s widely circulated publication, *Nostrums and Quackery*. Three years before, Miles and other company officials had been subjected to a fine under the food and drug laws for "misbranding."

Miles attended his last company board meeting at Elkhart in July 1924; the following year, though Miles retained the presidency of the company (until 1928), Andrew H. "Hub" Beardsley was, significantly, elected chairman of the board.

In just a few years, new ideas developed under Beardsley's leadership would bring the birth of Alka-Seltzer and a new "lease on life" for the company. Within a few decades, Miles would be completely transformed into an internationally known manufacturer of a wide spectrum of healthcare and industrial products. The Grand Dispensary, under pressure of growing criticism of its operations, closed in 1922.[60]

Despite many adversities, despite uncertain health, in their last years together Franklin and Elizabeth enjoyed many happy times in the house on First Street. They had lots of company: their children visited often, occupying the second floor of the First Street house and cottages at the farm. Louise, who married Donald Bass in February 1925, continued to spend much time attending to her parents' needs. The Miles celebrated the marriage of a grandchild and the births of their first great-grandchildren.

At last, disease combined with old age to sap his energy, and in the spring of 1928 Franklin Miles' poor health caused him to be confined to the house. His death about a year later, on the morning of April 1, 1929, was not unexpected.

An overflow crowd attended his funeral at the First Street house. Afterward his body was taken by train to be buried at Grace Lawn Cemetery in Elkhart, near the graves of his father, his grandmother, his first wife Ellen, and his daughter Frances. Long tributes appeared in the Fort Myers, Miami and Elkhart papers. Appreciative obituaries appeared also in drug trade publications.[61]

Elizabeth Miles lived on in the First Street house, joined by Louise and Donald Bass, until it, too, burned in 1940. Elizabeth State Miles died on October 2, 1941, at the age of seventy-five.[62]

Dr. Miles in Florida with his daughter Louise and grandchildren, about 1913; seated, l-r, Martha Elisabeth Miles, unidentified, Cathryn Collins, Louise Miles, Dr. Miles, John H. Collins, Jr.(standing), Edward Lawrence Miles (blurred), Charles Foster Miles, Franklin Beardsley Miles, Frank Miles Cleveland (very likely on the grounds of the "Shell House").

The "Shell House" with grounds and pier, at Miles farm, south of Fort Myers, ca. 1915; small figures include Dr. Miles (3rd from r).

Miles house on First Street, Fort Myers.

A late photograph of Dr. Miles, ca. 1923.

Harvesting green peppers at the Miles farm.

Barns at the Miles farm, south of Fort Myers, Florida.

One of many displays of Miles' Florida farm products.

Louise Miles with horse at the Miles farm, with the Caloosahatchee River in the background, ca. 1920.

7
Legacy

D r. Franklin Lawrence Miles brought into the world the Dr. Miles Medical Company and Dr. Miles' Nervine, a household necessity for generations. His corporate legacy beyond the early years of the company may never, perhaps, be fully understood, since others built up, developed and administered the firm, and many of the contributions he made in an advisory role do not appear in written records.

However, Dr. Donald N. Yates, formerly Miles archivist and supervisor of employee communications, wrote, "Long-lasting influences may be seen in the company's emphasis on analgesics and drugs for the nervous system, its use of attention-getting 'reason-why' advertising, and its sense of responsibility both to users of its products and to druggists. This began in Franklin Miles' era with competent business management, devices for customer information and 'feedback,' an awareness of social and legal accountability, and full-price marketing.

"The company, like the man, never shied away from controversy and often took roles ahead of its time and beyond the comprehension of local interests. Miles also put his imprint on the organization in a style of leadership that ensured a long tradition of rationalism, worldliness and entrepreneurial values."

Miles' potential contributions to medical science were diluted or sidetracked by his many-sided ambition and many-faceted interests. His hundreds of thousands of meticulously written and carefully organized records, which seem to have been totally destroyed, were never fully analyzed nor the results published in scholarly form.

However, his contributions to better popular health habits and better health awareness, not only as a physician but also as a writer, were certainly very great. Millions throughout the world used his medications and read the pamphlets written wholly or partly by him, and benefited from his advice. Though he was only one of many medical figures regularly issuing such advice, his name and image "stuck" in the public mind. It is worth noting that even the American Medical Association, decades later, established a popular health magazine, *Hygeia.*

His successful contribution on a smaller scale, as a builder of the Fort Myers region, is easy to document. Here, at last, he found the opportunity to be, all at the same time, a man in close touch with the earth and water, a pioneer and an innovator, a thorough investigator and educator, a wealthy and influential citizen, a generous benefactor, a patriarch of unquestioned authority, and a full-time "family man."

Of his legacy to his family and community, his great-granddaughter Susan Miles Yeckel describes a lasting tradition of altruism, modesty, humility. "His life was a testament to his selfless humanitarianism. His success and achievements only allowed him to serve his community in a greater capacity."

She continues, "It was with great love and affection that my father (Charles Foster Miles) always spoke of his grandfather. My father held him in loving high regard, with great respect and devotion. And this love and respect was evidenced in the correspondence of Dr. Miles and his children and grandchildren. Their love for him was a reflection of his love for them. I've never heard an unkind word spoken about him or attributed to him.

"He was the standard bearer—and those standards still exist. The strong sense of justice, love, devotion, family, inquiring minds, caring for others, humility, respect, I saw these characteristics in my aunts and uncles and I see them in my cousins today."

List of Names, Franklin L. Miles' Family

Grandparents
Laura Carter Miles Strong (1790-1864)
Erastus Miles (1783-1826)
Ralph Lawrence (1795-1845)
Sallie B. Satterlee Lawrence (1800—18??)

Parents
Charles Julius Miles (1820-1865)
Electa Lawrence Miles (c. 1822-1857)

Siblings
Kate Miles (c. 1847-1856)
Charles Miles (1851-1856)

Wives
Ellen Lighthall Miles (1851-1881)
Elizabeth State Miles (c. 1866-1941)

Children
Charles Franklin Miles (1875-1944)
Marian Miles Collins (1878-1946)
Electa Miles Cleveland Porter (1880-1932)
Frances Miles (c. 1895-1904)
Louise Miles Bass (ad. 1908) (c.1905—)

Grandchildren
Franklin Beardsley Miles (1905-1989)
Charles Foster Miles (1907-1989)
Martha Elisabeth Miles Crow 1908-1993)
Edward Lawrence Miles (1910-1985)
John Hyde Collins (1905-1924)

Cathryn Collins Keller (1908-19??)
Frank Miles Cleveland (c. 1900-19??)
Miles Bass (1926-1983)
Sidney Ann Bass Brinson (1938—)
James Bass (1941—)

Great-grandchildren
Franklin Beardsley Miles, Jr. (1939—)
Dorinda Miles Smith (1941—)
Susan Miles Yeckel (1939—)
Rachel Elisabeth Crow Dosé (1943—)
Florence Jeanette Crow Monger (1946—)
Lawrence Edward Miles (1938—)
William Foster Miles (1941—)
Kathlyn Keller Blackburn(1929-1989)
Carlie Cleveland (1927—)
Bruce Cleveland (1932—)
Melville Gibbons Brinson III (1961—)
Donald Lee Brinson (1963—)
Katherine Suzanne Brinson Clapp (1965—)
Jennifer Louise Bass (1975—)
Jeannie Rebecca Bass (1977—)

Notes

It is regrettable that Miles' two houses in Florida, which contained most of his personal papers and business records, were destroyed by fire. Records of his medical clinic and of his Florida "agricultural experiment station" also apparently were destroyed.

However, a few personal papers, saved by him and given to his children, have survived. These interesting items, which give insights into his thought processes, are still owned by his descendants. Photocopies of items from one such group are in a notebook at the Miles Archives at Bayer Corporation in Elkhart.

In the Miles Archives, too, is a wealth of material pertaining to the early history of the Dr. Miles Medical Company, including early advertising publications, medical labels, early account books, minutes and other records. There also are a few items from the Dr. Miles Grand Dispensary.

Recollections of his descendants, now at the Miles Archives and Fort Myers Historical Museum, document his family life. Personal letters in the Beardsley family archives at Ruthmere Museum in Elkhart help "flesh out" Miles' last years. Newspapers in Elkhart County and Fort Myers detail many of his activities.

Records of government and private agencies, such as the U.S. Patent Office, American Medical Association, Elkhart County Medical Association, Elkhart County Auditor and Elkhart Museum Association (the last two at the Elkhart County Historical Society), and Lee County (Florida) Recorder provide vital clues.

Many of the sources cited below are available in the Miles Archives, in original, photocopy, or abstract form.

Preface

1. William C. Cray, *Miles: A Centennial History* (Englewood, N.J.:Prentice-Hall, 1984).

Epigraph Page

1. Part of a reprinted quote from *The Craftsman*, No. 2, 1902, found in Miles/Hamlin genealogy compiled by Lucretia Belle Hamlin, now owned by Susan Miles Yeckel. Probably by Bishop John Lancaster Spalding (1840-1916), a prominent Catholic writer.

Chapter 1

1. Franklin Miles' height was estimated by his grandson Charles Foster Miles at 5´2´´. (Interview Notes, 1975, Research Notebooks on Miles, Miles Archives, hereafter designated simply as Research Notebooks.) Charles Foster Miles' daughter, Susan Miles Yeckel, stresses that short stature was not considered to be of importance by the family.

From here on in these notes, Dr. Franklin L. Miles will be referred to as "Miles."

2. Bill Rich, notes on Miles, Research Notebooks.

3. Miles' use of Chesterfield: Louise Miles Bass, Interview Notes, Research Notebooks.

Chapter 2

1. The date Nov. 15, 1845, given in Miles' obituaries may be incorrect--or guesswork. The 1850 Federal Census of Elyria, Ohio, lists Miles' age as six. In a letter of Miles to Samuel Strong, Aug. 4, 1868, Miles refers to age twenty-three as an earlier age (Letter Book in Miles Personal Papers, copies in notebook, Miles Archives—designated hereafter as Miles Personal Papers).

An even less likely birth date of Nov. 15, 1847 appears on his April 1865 registration card at Phillips Academy, Andover, Massachusetts, but is contradicted by a notation, "age 19." The later birth date also appears in a biographical sketch in *Unrivalled Chicago* (Chicago: Rand McNally, 1896), p. 117. The 1910 Federal Census of Fort Myers, Florida lists Miles as sixty-three. Early biographical sketches avoid giving a birth date, but sometimes list events of his life on the basis of the 1847 date: George W. Butler, *The Manual of Elkhart* (Elkhart: Mennonite Publishing Co., 1889), unnumbered page; *Pictorial and Biographical Memoirs of Elkhart and St. Joseph Counties, Indiana* (Chicago: Goodspeed Bros., 1893), p. 28-29; Anthony Deahl, *Twentieth Century History and Biographical Record of Elkhart County, Indiana* (Chicago: Lewis Publishing Co., 1905), p. 420-23; and Abraham E. Weaver, *A Standard History of Elkhart County, Indiana* (Chicago: American Historical Society, 1916), v. 2, p. 424-27.

2. The importance given by Miles to his ancestors is indicated by descriptions in Deahl, *Twentieth Century History*, p. 420-21; in his obituaries (*Elkhart Truth*, Apr. 1, 1929, *Fort Myers Tropical News,* Apr. 2, 1929, and *Fort Myers Evening Press,* Apr. 1, 1929); and other biographical sketches. Other sources for family history include a genealogy compiled for Miles by his cousin, Lucretia Belle Hamlin (now owned by Miles' great-granddaughter, Susan Miles Yeckel of Dallas, Texas); Lemuel E. Hamlin, "The Hamlin Family," formerly owned by a granddaughter, the late Elisabeth Miles Crow; biographical sketches of his son Charles Franklin Miles and Marian Miles

Collins (Citizen's Historical Assn., Indianapolis, 1948); and interviews with Elisabeth Miles Crow (Interview Notes, Research Notebooks).

3. Charles Julius Miles may have made more than one trip west. He was not listed with his wife Electa and her children in the 1850 Federal Census of Elyria; however, records of the Cemetery of Spring Grove, Cincinnati, show Franklin Miles' younger brother Charles to have been born Sept. 20, 1851 at Columbus. Records in the State of Hawaii Archives, Honolulu, confirm Charles Julius Miles' official appointment Dec. 1, 1855, and his departure in November, 1860 (copies in Research Notebooks).

4. *Famous Men and Women,* 1896, Miles Archives.

5. Letters from Miles to Edward Stow Hamlin, Jan. 5, 1867; to Samuel Strong, Aug. 4, 1868, Letter Book, Miles Personal Papers.

6. Records of Cemetery of Spring Grove (Sec. 79, lot 53) list death dates of May 30 and Dec. 28, 1856, and Jan. 13, 1857. A family story that all three died in an epidemic may be partly true, considering the closeness of the latter two deaths.

7. Miles to Edward Stow Hamlin, Jan. 5, 1867 and to A. G. Lawrence, Feb. 22, 1867, Letter Book, Miles Personal Papers.

8. Miles' comments on his personality development in letter to Edward Stow Hamlin, Jan. 5, 1867, Letter Book, Miles Personal Papers.

9. There is uncertainty about Miles' place of residence after his mother's death. The Miles, Lawrence, Strong and Hamlin families were interconnected by multiple marriages. The uncle and aunt described by Miles to his daughter (Bass, Memoirs, p. 8, in Oral Histories, Miles Archives, hereafter referred to simply as Memoirs) may possibly have been one of the following:

a. A. G. Lawrence and his wife, of Adrian, Mich. Perhaps the most likely, since Miles was living with him sometime between about 1862 and 1864. (Charles Julius Miles to Franklin Miles, undated, Letter Book, Miles Personal Papers).

b. Lorenzo and Myra Lawrence Miles, his father's brother and mother's sister, who are said to have lived in Michigan (Louise Miles Bass, Videotape, 1984, Miles Archives).

c. Edward Stow Hamlin and his second wife, Mary Eliza Strong (who was a daughter of Miles' grandmother, Laura Carter Miles, and her second husband, James Strong of Cleveland). Miles' daughter's Memoirs refer to a farm, which might be Hamlin's in Massachusetts. Miles later spent much time there.

d. Samuel and Louisa Strong of Elkhart. Samuel Strong was a nephew of James Strong; Louisa Strong, Samuel's wife, was his cousin, another daughter of James and Laura Carter Miles Strong.

e. Lewis W. Pickering, of Elkhart, and his wife, Frances Strong Pickering (a third daughter of Miles' grandmother through her second marriage). There were other aunts and uncles as well.

10. Charles Julius Miles' Hawaiian letters were saved by his son, reportedly in

later years in a company safe, but have disappeared (Louise Miles Bass, Memoirs, 1983, p. 9). Charles Julius Miles' departure from Hawaii: see Note 3.

11. A business partnership between Charles Julius Miles and Samuel Strong in Elkhart is documented in the *Goshen* (Indiana) *Express,* Oct. 21, 1837. Miles and Strong had accounts with merchant Elijah Beardsley (Store Ledger, #77.14.680, p. 19-21, Elkhart County Historical Society Archives). Miles did some work for Beardsley. Miles' grandmother (d. 1864) is buried near her son Charles Julius Miles at Grace Lawn Cemetery, Elkhart, but since her husband, James Strong, later appeared to be a resident of Cleveland, according to a biographical sketch of Samuel Strong in *History of Elkhart County Indiana* (Chicago: Charles C. Chapman & Co., 1881, p. 868), it is not known if Laura Carter Miles Strong resided in Elkhart for a length of time. She cannot be found in the 1860 Federal Census of Elkhart.

12. Miles' living in Elkhart: see *Pictorial and Biographical Memoirs,* p. 28; Weaver, *Standard History of Elkhart County,* which states, "He has been more or less closely identified with the city since 1861" (p. 424). Also in Bass, Memoirs, p. 7; Elisabeth Miles Crow, Interview Notes, 1975, Research Notebooks. About 1861 Charles wrote his brother Lorenzo: "Frank is with us, and well. A good boy." His letter to Franklin Jan. 27, 1865 confirms his son helped in the store (Miles Personal Papers). Boyhood boating described in *Elkhart Review,* undated clipping, Research Notebooks.

13. Charles Julius Miles to Franklin Miles, undated, May 30, 1864, Sept. 20, 1864, Miles Personal Papers. The Hamlin farm was perhaps 30 miles from Williston, near the New York state line, west of Lenox (Franklin B. Miles, Memoirs, p. 5; Elisabeth Miles Crow, Interview Notes, 1975, Research Notebooks).

14. Quotes from letters, Charles Julius Miles to Miles, Jan. 27, 1865, Oct. 20, 1864, Miles Personal Papers.

15. An entry in Miles' Autograph Book (Miles Personal Papers) indicates his eyes were a problem as late as 1869. Miles' letters to Hamlin, Jan. 5, 1867; to A. G. Lawrence, Feb. 13, 1867; to Samuel Strong, Aug. 4, 1868 (Letter Book, Miles Personal Papers) establish the other conditions. It may be that his early choices of schools were strongly influenced by Hamlin.

16. Miles is listed in *The Twenty-Fourth Annual Catalogue of Williston Seminary* (Northampton, Mass., 1865). Williston and its headmaster are described in Joseph H. Sawyer, *A History of Williston Seminary* (Northampton: Williston Trustees, 1917), and "Athletics in Williston's First One Hundred Years," *Holyoke Transcript,* June 6, 1941.

17. Autograph Book, Miles Personal Papers. This inscription and another autograph refer to "Hull's Hotel," apparently a lodging place for some of the students.

18. Miles is listed in Andover's annual catalogues for 1865 and 1866. Andover is described in *An Andover Primer: Phillips Academy and Its History 1778-1928*

(Andover: Phillips Academy, 1928). The "canning" story could not be confirmed by archivists at either Andover or Williston. Letters and Autograph Book, Miles Personal Papers, contain items pertaining to friends including E. F. Russel and a "Miss Sanborn."

19. Miles to A. G. Lawrence, Feb. 22, 1867, Letter Book, Miles Personal Papers. Miles' youthful experience in horsemanship from working on his uncle's farm is mentioned by Bass (Memoirs, p. 7). She also recalls his saying he was president of a collegiate rifle and pistol club (Memoirs, p. 5). In old age, he taught Louise to box (Bass, Interview Notes, p. 6, Research Notebooks).

20. The *Elkhart Review* gives Charles' death date as May 5, 1865. His store stock was bought by a Maj. C. B. Monahan *(Elkhart Review,* Aug. 12, 1865). Financial matters discussed in letters to A. G. Lawrence, Samuel Strong, Edward Stow Hamlin, Letter Book, Miles Personal Papers. Spending inheritance mentioned in Bass, Memoirs, p. 8. Properties in Cleveland apparently had been inherited by Miles.

21. *Second Annual Report of the Sheffield Scientific School of Yale College, 1866-7* (New Haven, 1867); Brooks Mather Kelley, *Yale-A History,* p. 248-64; Russell H. Chittenden, *History of the Sheffield Scientific School* (New Haven, 1928).

22. Miles letters to A. G. Lawrence and E. S. Hamlin, Jan.-Feb. 1867, Letter Book, Miles Personal Papers.

23. Miles to A. G. Lawrence, Feb. 22, 1867, Letter Book, Miles Personal Papers.

24. Miles to Samuel Strong, Aug. 4, 1868, Letter Book, Miles Personal Papers. His letters confirm his location, though Sheffield records list him only in 1866-67. Yale archivists suggest he may have been a private student of zoologist Addison Verrill.

25. Miles to "Austin," Apr. 1, 1869; biographical sketches and library catalog, Letter Book, Miles Personal Papers.

26. Miles to unnamed woman friend, Sept. 1, 1868, Letter Book, Miles Personal Papers.

27. He described this experience in his article "The Davenport Brothers," *Elkhart Observer,* Dec. 18, 1872. Opinions in essay, "Mediums," in Letter Book, Miles Personal Papers.

28. Miles to "A," c. Early 1869, Letter Book, Miles Personal Papers. This would have been a mainstream opinion in 1869.

29. Autograph book; Miles to "A," c. early 1869 and to unnamed woman, Sept. 1, 1868, Letter Book, Miles Personal Papers.

30. Miles to Samuel Strong, Aug. 4, 1868, Letter Book, Miles Personal Papers. Miles claimed that Hamlin wanted to get his hands on some of the family funds.

31. Miles to unnamed woman, Sept. 1, 1868, Letter Book, Miles Personal Papers.

32. Miles to "Austin," Apr. 1, 1869, Letter Book, Miles Personal Papers.

33. The fish farm may never have been actually developed; the Letter Book shows no evidence that it was. Miles' earlier references to "argumentation" may foreshadow his decision to study law. Hamlin's influence also might have been a factor in that decision.

34. Miles is listed in the *Annual Catalog of Yale College 1869-70* (New Haven, 1869); the law school in his era is described in *Celebration of the School of Law Yale University 16 June 1924* (New Haven, 1924) p. 10-12.

35. "Connecticut Divorce Law," Letter Book, Miles Personal Papers.

36. Described in *A History of the School of Law, Columbia University* (New York: Columbia University Press, 1955), p. 60-61. In later years Miles claimed the title LL.B., saying he had completed the course but was unwilling to pay a graduation fee. Columbia's records list him as a non-graduating student (1871).

37. Notes on "Propagation Business," Letter Book, Miles Personal Papers.

38. Bass, Memoirs, p. 8.

39. Reprinted in *Human Rights: A Quarterly Journal for the People* (Elkhart: Mennonite Publishing Co., 1888), p. 2-4.

40. "Propagation Business," Letter Book, Miles Personal Papers. Harvard's archives cannot verify the study with Agassiz.

41. "Modes of Making Money," Letter Book, Miles Personal Papers.

42. "Propagation Business," Letter Book, Miles Personal Papers.

43. "Advertising," Letter Book, Miles Personal Papers.

44. "Advertising," Letter Book, Miles Personal Papers. In 1888, Miles corresponded with Barnum, and kept Barnum's letters for his descendants (copies in Miles Personal Papers).

45. Bass, Memoirs, p. 8.

46. Miles is listed in the school catalog for 1871-72.

47. William G. Rothstein, *American Physicians in the Nineteenth Century: From Sects to Science* (Baltimore: Johns Hopkins Press, 1972), p. 289.

48. Burke A. Hinsdale, *History of the University of Michigan* (Ann Arbor, University of Michigan, 1906), p. 90-94, 226. The Palmer letter, published repeatedly in Miles' early advertising literature (an example: *The Dr. Miles Medical and Ocular Institute, for the Special Treatment of Serious and Complicated Chronic Nervous and Eye Diseases,* Elkhart: Review Printing Co., 1893, p. 23) is dated "February 1871." Possibly it should read "February 1872." Another course he took at Michigan may have been "Practical Anatomy" (medical school attendance cards, Miles Personal Papers).

49. Edward C. Atwater, "Internal Medicine," in Ronald L. Numbers (ed.), *The Education of American Physicians* (Berkeley: University of California Press, 1980); p. 144-50; Charles Rosenberg, "The Practice of Medicine in New York a Century Ago" (1967) in Judith W. Leavitt and Ronald L. Numbers (eds.), *Sickness and Health in America* (Madison: Univ. of Wisconsin, 1978), p. 63; John H. Warner, *The Therapeutic Perspective: Medical Practice, Knowledge, Identity in America 1820-80* (Cambridge: Harvard University Press, 1986), p. 202. The Flint textbook is full of Miles'

pencilled notes, especially plentiful in the sections on lung diseases.

50. Harrington is listed as Miles' preceptor in *Thirty-Second Annual Announcement, Rush Medical College, 1874-75* (Chicago, 1874), p. 16. No other references to Miles' study with Harrington could be found. Miles was living in Elkhart between medical school sessions. There appears to be no record of his attendance at a medical school in 1872-73. Harrington's medical degree is listed in Elkhart County Clerk, Physicians' License Record, 1885-97, p. 10, Elkhart County Historical Society Archives. Harrington advertisements in *Elkhart Review,* Feb. 6 and Apr. 7, 1869; Dec. 12, 1872.

51. *Elkhart Observer,* Oct. 2, 1872; Nov. 6, 1872; Dec. 18, 1872.

52. *Ibid.* Apr. 23, 1873.

53. Obituary of Ellen Miles, *Elkhart Review,* Aug. 25, 1881; letter from Candia (?) Birdsall to Miss Hamlin (Aug. 21, 1916), copy in Research Notebooks; 1870 Federal Census of Elkhart; *Elkhart Observer,* Jan. 14, 1874, Jan. 21, Aug. 19, 1874. According to items in Miles Personal Papers, Ellen Miles attended Hahnemann Medical College in 1873-74 and Woman's Hospital Medical College in 1874-75. She studied obstetrics among other subjects at both schools and received a certificate for passing an examination Feb. 25, 1875 from the Chicago Women's Medical College.

54. *Elkhart Observer,* Sept. 3, Sept. 24, Oct. 1, Oct. 8, Oct. 15 and Oct. 22, 1873.

55. Why Miles changed from Michigan to Rush is not known. He is listed as a Feb. 1874 graduate of Rush in Physicians' License Record, p. 9, Elkhart County Historical Society Archives; Rush Medical College Student Matriculation Book, Rush-Presbyterian-St. Luke's Medical Center Archives, Chicago; and *Chicago Medical Journal,* v. 31 (1874), p. 319. Rush Medical College at this period is described in *Thirty-First Annual Announcement of Rush Medical College, 1873-74* (Chicago, 1873); Stanton A. Friedberg, M. D., "History of Laryngology in Early Chicago and Rush Medical College," *Annals of Otology, Rhinology and Laryngology,* v. 88 (1979), p. 136-40, and Ernest E. Irons, *Story of Rush Medical College* (Chicago: Rush Medical College, 1953); Atwater, "Internal Medicine," in *The Education of American Physicians,* p. 154.

56. Medical school attendance cards, Miles Personal Papers.

57. *Chicago Medical Journal,* v. 31 (1874), p. 193-206.

58. *Elkhart Observer,* May 6, 1874; *Dr. Miles Neuropathic Cure...*(Chicago: Dr. Miles Association, 1902), p. 14.

59. Rothstein, *American Physicians in the Nineteenth Century,* p. 207-211; Charles Rosenberg, *The Structure of American Medical Practice 1875-1941* (Philadelphia: University of Pennsylvania Press, 1983), p. 81-87; Rosenberg, "Practice of Medicine in New York a Century Ago," *Sickness and Health in America,* p. 65-66.

60. Though his attendance is not shown in surviving records of Northwestern University Medical School, successor to Chicago Medical College, Miles' early pub-

lications consistently list Chicago Medical College as one of his "credentials," and carry a later letter from editor Jewell showing interest in Miles' discoveries. (Among others, *The Dr. Miles Medical and Ocular Institute*, p. 23.) Also, among Miles Personal Papers, there is a matriculation ticket to Chicago Medical College, Oct. 1874. The College's pre-eminence in medical education is stressed by Martin Kaufman in "American Medical Education," *Education of American Physicians*, p. 15. Rush's use of the Chicago Medical College facilities after the Great Fire is mentioned in Irons, *Story of Rush Medical College*, p. 26.

61. Barbara Sicherman, "The Uses of a Diagnosis: Doctors, Patients and Neurasthenia," reprinted in *Sickness and Health in America*, p. 25-38. Works by Beard and Mitchell are mentioned in a number of Miles' early publications.

62. *Thirty-First Annual Announcement, Rush Medical College*, p. 7; *Annual Report, Chicago Charitable Eye & Ear Infirmary*, year ending Nov. 30, 1874 (Chicago, 1874); Friedberg, *op. cit.*, p. 136. The letter from Holmes is in *The Dr. Miles Medical and Ocular Institute*, p. 23, among others. Two courses did not necessarily represent a thorough study of the subject in 1875, but no criteria for practice as an ophthalmalogist had been established (Rosenberg, *The Structure of American Medical Practice*, p. 83), and judging from his later success as a specialist and surgeon, Miles must have applied himself intensely to his studies.

63. Mitchell is mentioned by Miles in his only known medical journal article, "Ocular Irritation a Cause of Nasal Afflictions," *Weekly Medical Review of St. Louis*, 1884, 111-12. Key articles by S. Weir Mitchell, M. D., include "Headaches, from Heat-Stroke, from Fevers, after Meningitis, from Over Use of Brain, from Eye Strain," *Medical and Surgical Reporter*, v. 31 (1874), p. 67-70, 81-84; "Notes on Headaches," v. 32 (1875), p. 101-04; "Headaches from Eye Strain," *American Journal of Medical Sciences*, v. 71 (1876), p. 363-73. Miles agrees with Mitchell in seeing the eye as the culprit in many cases of headache and other nervous disorders.

A chronology of Miles' investigation of the nervous system is given in a biographical sketch, possibly written by himself, in *Pictorial and Biographical Memoirs of Elkhart and St. Joseph Counties Indiana*, p. 28: "In 1873 he began to study the relationship between the brain and eye and the brain and heart, and in time could trace the effect of the one upon the other. Understanding his subject he traced diseases to first causes and effected some most extraordinary cures. In 1875 he took up the subject of the heart with the same result..." The article describes his study of the eyes at the Infirmary as "prosecuting the closest study of those delicate organs and reasoning for himself the dependence of each on the other and on the whole human system."

64. For Ellen Miles' course of study, see note 53. Also among Miles' papers is a blank commencement certificate from Hahnemann, (1875), which could be Ellen's (Miles Personal Papers). In addition to his conventional medical studies, Miles too may have sampled the offerings of the Homeopathic and/or Eclectic medical sects.

A brief notice in the *Elkhart Observer* (Jan. 21, 1874) reported that he would take an "eclectic course." A 1976 letter from the Northwestern Memorial Hospital Archives, Chicago, indicates that Miles may have taken a course at Hahnemann Medical College during 1872. This could not, however, be confirmed in later correspondence with the archivist.

Chapter 3

1. *Elkhart Observer,* May 12, May 26, 1875; *Elkhart Review,* May 20,1875.

2. For the history of Elkhart at this period, see Emil V. Anderson, *Taproots of Elkhart History* (Elkhart: Truth Publishing Co., 1970 reprint) p. 29-49; Butler, *Manual of Elkhart;* Polly Bentley, *Jottings from the Sedate Eighties and the Gay Nineties* (Elkhart, 1938); *History of Elkhart County,* Indiana (Chapman); Martha M. Pickrell, *Women in Elkhart a Century Ago* (Elkhart, 1978); Elkhart City Directories, 1874, 1883, 1885-86.

3. *Elkhart Observer,* June 16, 1875, June 30, 1875; *Elkhart Review,* June 21, 1877; Physicians License Record, 1885-97, Elkhart County Historical Society Archives, gives medical school and year of graduation.

4. *Elkhart Review,* July 28, 1875.

5. *Ibid.,* Sept. 14, 1875.

6. *Ibid.* May 4 or 11, 1876.

7. A photocopy of this early scholarly pamphlet is in the Miles Archives. There is also a brief description of it in the *Elkhart Review,* April 27, 1876. An early description of the frequent practice of publishing articles and treatises to attract business appears in *Journal of the American Medical Association,* v. 2 (1884), p. 652-55.

8. *Elkhart Review,* Feb. 21, 1878, August 1, 1878; Elkhart County Auditor, Commissioners' Papers, Sept. and Dec. terms 1877, in Elkhart County Historical Society Archives; *Elkhart Review,* April 26, 1877.

9. *Ibid.* Dec. 20, 1877. Also, a new office in the "Old Elkhart Bank" mentioned in the *Elkhart Review,* May 15, 1879.

10. *Ibid.* June 27, 1878, Oct. 24, 1878.

11. The full extent of Ellen Miles' practice is not known. This brief period is the only time her advertisement appears in the *Review.*

12. Gravestones, Grace Lawn Cemetery, Elkhart. (Records at Rice Cemetery.)

13. Items concerning the city museum appear in the *Elkhart Review,* May 2, 1878; April 10, May 8, June 5 and June 26, 1879; Feb. 5 and Aug. 5, 1880; *History of Elkhart County* (Chapman), p. 740. Historical information was gathered as well (*Review,* May 8, 1879). Museum record in Miles' handwriting, Elkhart County Historical Society Archives; copy in Miles Personal Papers.

14. *Elkhart Review,* Jan. 15, 1880.

15. Minutes, Elkhart County Medical Association, 1878-84, kept by the secretary. Cases mentioned here appear on p. 33 (Apr. 13, 1880); p. 40 (Dec. 14, 1880); p. 42 (Feb. 8, 1881); p. 51 (Feb. 14, 1882); p. 26 (Oct. 14, 1879); p. 36 (June 15, 1880); p. 46 (June 14, 1881); p. 48 (Oct. 11, 1881). Miles joined the Indiana State Medical Society in September 1882, according to *Transactions of the Indiana State Medical Society*, v. 32 (1882), p. 295.

16. Out-of-town eye and ear patients are described in *Elkhart Review*, Feb. 12, 1880, May 6, 1880, Oct. 12, 1882, Nov. 1, 1883; other types of cases, *Ibid.* Aug. 12, 1880, Dec. 24, 1881, Apr. 13, 1882, Aug. 3, 1882. Vaccination is mentioned in *Ibid.* Apr. 10, 1879, Jan. 19, 1882. Bass' father told of returning from night calls asleep in his buggy; the horses knew the way (Bass, Videotape).

17. Articles concerning the Elkhart City Board of Health, sanitation problems, etc. appear in the *Elkhart Review*, July 8, July 29 and Nov. 18, 1880, Jan. 20, 1881, and Mar. 23, 1882. The exchange of letters with Kremer is in the *Elkhart Daily Review*, May 7, May 9, May 11, May 12, and May 13, 1881.

Chapter 4

1. *Elkhart Review*, Aug. 25, 1881.

2. Bass, Memoirs, p. 8; Bass, Videotape; Elisabeth Miles Crow, Interview Notes, 1975 and 1985, Research Notebooks.

3. For example, in 1882, when some of his contemporaries were erecting spacious houses, Miles had his residence and office on the second floor of a building on West Jackson Blvd. nearly opposite the Post Office (*Elkhart Review*, Jan. 10, 1922) and remained there until about 1885, when he lived at 314 W. Pigeon St., now Lexington Ave. (Elkhart City Directories) These must have been rented quarters, since deed records do not record a purchase. The *South Bend Tribune*, June 29, 1881, shows him advertising his services one day a week in that city. Miles' position for the insurance company is noted in *Elkhart Review*, Sept. 24, 1885. Competition in the medical practice of the era: Rosenberg, *Structure of American Medical Practice*, p. 19-20, 24.

Excerpts from A.M.A. Code of Ethics (in *Journal of the American Medical Association*, v. II (1884), p. 709: "It is derogatory to the dignity of the profession to resort to public advertisements...inviting the attention of individuals afflicted with particular diseases...to adduce certificates of skill and success...these are the ordinary practice of empirics...Equally derogatory to professional character is it for a physician to hold a patent for any surgical instrument or medicine, or to dispense a secret nostrum...It is also reprehensible for physicians to give certificates attesting the efficacy of patent or secret medicines, or in any way to promote the use of them."

4. Biographical sketch in Butler, *Manual of Elkhart*, unnumbered page(1889).

5. There are no records to verify tuberculosis. Poor health is cited as a reason

for Miles' move to Florida in his obituaries and in Bass, Memoirs, p. 10; Bass, Videotape; Bass, Interview Notes, 1985, p. 1, Research Notebooks; and Edward L. Miles, Memoirs, p. 4. A hiatus in Miles' advertising from January to August, 1884 (*Elkhart Sentinel*) might possibly indicate sickness. His frail health in about 1894 was described by Bob Holland, a former employee, in an article in the *Miami Herald,* Apr. 2, 1929.

6. *Elkhart Daily Sentinel,* Aug. 11, 1884. References to studies by Beard, Jewell, Mitchell and others appear often in Miles' publications.

7. For discussion of these problems and procedures as understood by an eminent physician, see S. Weir Mitchell, publications cited in Chapter 2, Note 63.

8. *Weekly Medical Review of St. Louis,* 1884, p. 111-12.

9. *The Dr. Miles Medical and Ocular Institute* (1893), p. 23, among others.

10. *Human Rights, A Quarterly Journal for the People...* (Elkhart, 1888), p. 2.

11. No. 339,676, filed Aug. 26, 1885, Serial No. 175,392; described in *Specifications and Drawings of Patents Issued from the United States Patent Office* (Washington: U.S. Government Printing Office, 1886), p. 857-58.

12. Label registration papers for Dr. Miles' Restorative Nervine, also recorded in *Official Gazette, U.S. Patent Office* (Washington, D.C. v. 22, 1882), p. 180, are in the Miles Archives. Early sales and expenses are recorded in Miles' Account Book, 1882-86, also in the Miles Archives. Miles' development of Dr. Miles' Restorative Nervine is described in *New and Startling Facts For Those Afflicted with Nervous Diseases* (Elkhart: Dr. Miles Medical Co., c. 1891), p. 2, and *The Dr. Miles Medical and Ocular Institute,* p. 10. The word "nervine" was far from original with Miles; it was a generic term for nerve medicines.

13. Charles S. Beardsley, address, Miles Laboratories Sales Convention, 1948, p. 12, in Miles Archives; Bass, Memoirs, p. 12.

14. Product descriptions were written in 1954 by Harry W. Beaver, who supervised production for nearly 50 years. None, however, was written on Nervine. Production records kept by Beaver started in 1910. A contemporary piece on bromides that Miles may have read is E. C. Seguin, M.D., "The Abuse and Use of Bromides," *Journal of Nervous and Mental Diseases,* v. 4 (1877), p. 445-61. The story of Miles' use of Fowler's solution in Nervine has been handed down in the family (see Charles Foster Miles, Interview Notes, 1975, Research Notebooks). The addition of Fowler's solution is recommended by Dr. George A. Beard in *A Practical Treatise on Nervous Exhaustion* (New York: William Wood & Co., 1880), p. 154, which Miles no doubt read since he quotes the book in *Human Rights,* p. 17 and *The Dr. Miles Medical and Ocular Institute,* p. 8.

15. Bass, Memoirs, p. 12.

16. *The Dr. Miles Medical and Ocular Institute,* p. 10.

17. Warner, T*he Therapeutic Perspective,* p. 100-19, 250, 267-68. James Harvey Young, *The Toadstool Millionaires* (Princeton: Princeton University Press, 1961), p. 93-202; Charles E. Rosenberg, "Practice of Medicine in New York a Century Ago," *Sickness and Health in America,* p. 63-65. Another factor might have been the lack of

licensing of pharmacists in Indiana until 1899: Glenn L. Jenkins, "Hoosier Pharmacy: An Historical Sketch," in Dorothy Russo, ed., *100 Years of Indiana Medicine* (Indianapolis: Indiana State Medical Assn., 1949).

18. *New and Startling Facts For Those Afflicted With Nervous Diseases*, p. 6. This position is evident in many of Miles' early company publications. In *Dr. Miles' Medical Monthly* (Dr. Miles Medical Co., 1894), p. 3, he writes, "...while Dr. Franklin Miles has nothing whatever to do with the manufacture or sale of proprietary medicines, he supplies to this stock company the formulas from which they are made . . ."

19. For notices and advertisements for these companies, see *Elkhart Review*, Feb. 27, 1879 (Bucklen); Feb. 7, 1884 (Chamberlain); Oct. 18, 1883 and July 23, 1885 (Jones & Primley).

20. Miles, Account Book, 1882-86, Miles Archives; *Elkhart Review*, Apr. 24, 1884. No *Medical News* issues have survived.

21. Miles, Account Book, 1882-84.

22. Notes on interview with Jack Linton, Research Notebooks.

23. Articles of Association of the Dr. Miles Medical Co., filed Nov. 6, 1885 with the Indiana Secretary of State, signed before the Elkhart County Recorder Oct. 28, 1885 (Misc. Record, V. 4, p. 19, Elkhart County Recorder).

24. Characterizations of these remedies are from *New and Startling Facts*, p. 2; ingredients from Harry W. Beaver, product descriptions. Ingredients in the Blood Purifier included *trifolium, stillingia* (Queen's delight), *phytolacca* (poke), *lappa* (burdock), *biberis aquifolium* (Oregon grape root), *cascara amarga* (Honduras bark), and *xanthoxylum* (prickly ash). Miles was already distributing some sort of "pills" to druggists in May 1884, according to his Account Book, 1882-86. However, the label for Dr. Miles' Restorative Nerve and Liver Pills was registered in July, 1887. Registration papers for the pills, also listed in *Official Gazette of the U.S. Patent Office*, v. 40, p. 122, are also in the Miles Archives. Beaver's product history (1954) notes that the pills were furnished by Parke Davis; Dr. Miles Medical Co., Minutes, v. 1, p. 2, Dec. 11, 1890, Miles Archives, record a decision to order "sugar coated pills from Upjohn, Kalamazoo." The name of the pills was later changed to Little Pills—a name often used by practitioners of Homeopathy. In regard to the current belief that the blood needed to be purified to remove infections, see Rosenberg, "The Practice of Medicine in New York a Century Ago," *Sickness and Health in America*, p. 70, Note 22.

25. Dr. Miles Medical Co., Minutes, v. 1, p. 1-3, Nov. 10, 1885.

26. Dr. Miles Medical Co. First Cash Book, 1885-88. Early locations, moves of the company are described in the small booklet, *A Brief History of Miles Laboratories, Inc.* (Elkhart: Miles Laboratories, Inc., 1938), and *New and Startling Facts*, p. 5.

27. Change of ownership described in Dr. Miles Medical Co., Minutes, v. 1, p. 8, Feb. 11-12, 1887. Burns' role is noted in the *Elkhart Review*, Feb. 17, 1887, and detailed in the Dr. Miles Medical Co. First Cash Book, 1885-88. Minutes, v. 1,

p. 17, May 19, 1890, show his activities being limited to compounding and bottling. Later estimate of George Compton's contribution to the company in Interview with Walter A. Compton, M.D., Oct. 14, 1980 (Indiana University Oral History Research Project), Oral History Collection, Miles Archives. Members of the Compton family continued to be involved both as board members and as administrators.

28. Dr. Miles Medical Co., First Cash Book, 1885-88. The first placement of newspaper advertisements is recorded Sept. 1, 1887. In October, advertisements appeared in such local papers as the *Goshen News, Goshen Times,* and *Elkhart Sentinel.*

29. Label registration papers, dated July 12, 1887 (also listed in *Official Gazette of the U. S. Patent Office,* v. 40, p. 122). Product description by Harry W. Beaver.

30. *Elkhart Review,* Feb. 16, 1888; Dr. Miles Medical Co., Second Cash Book, 1888-91.

31. Dr. Miles Medical Co., Minutes, v. 1, p. 12, Aug. 14, 1889; *Elkhart Review,* Aug. 22, 1889. A. R. Burns, whose interest had been purchased, was no longer part of the firm.

32. Documented in company Minutes, Cash Books, Journals, and Payroll Books, 1889-92. The Second Cash Book (1889-90) shows a jump in number of employees, salesmen, and sales.

33. Dr. Miles Medical Co., Minutes, v. 1, p. 21-22, Mar. 28 and May 9, 1892.

34. *Ibid.,* v. 1, p. 18, Dec. 11, 1890. For product prices see *New and Startling Facts,* p. 2.

35. *Elkhart Review,* June 18, 1891. View of offices appears in *Modern Miracles* (Elkhart: Dr. Miles Medical Co., 1893).

36. *Official Gazette of the U.S. Patent Office,* v. 23, p. 1930.

37. Dr. Miles Medical Co., Second Cash Book, May 4 - Oct. 26, 1889; Elkhart city directories, 1890, 1893-94; Bass, Memoirs, p. 2-3, 11. According to Louise Bass, Elizabeth State did proof-reading for a German newspaper in Elkhart (the only one being the *Herald of Truth,* published by the Mennonite Publishing Co.) before coming to work for Miles. Early Dr. Miles Medical Co. financial records and those of the Mennonite Publishing Co (Funk papers, Archives of the Mennonite Church, Goshen College) show that the Mennonite Publishing Co., which also offered job printing, did much of the medical company's early printing and advertising, along with the job printing department of the *Review.*

38. *Elkhart Review,* June 18, 1891; April 6, 1882, June 19, 1884, July 31, 1884, May 28, 1885, April 26, 1888, July 4, 1889.

39. *Human Rights,* p. 1-2. City living was a culprit in much current health literature; see Rosenberg, "The Practice of Medicine in New York a Century Ago," *Sickness and Health in America,* p. 55-56.

40. *Human Rights,* p. 5-8. The latter article reprinted from *Chicago Tribune,*

written Aug. 12, 1874. Mortality rates also mentioned in Rosenberg, "Practice of Medicine," *Sickness and Health in America,* p. 55.

41. *Ibid.* p. 14; *Elkhart Review,* Dec. 8, 1887.

42. *Human Rights..* p. 10.

43. *Ibid.* p. 11-12.

44. *Ibid.* p. 13-14.

45. *Ibid.* p. 15-17.

46. *Elkhart Review,* Apr. 19, 1888, June 7, 1888, June 14, 1888. Since only scattered issues of Miles' publications have survived, it is often hard to tell how many issues there were. Correspondence with Barnum is in Miles Personal Papers.

47. *New and Startling Facts,* p. 27. This publication was a company staple, and may have been revised a number of times.

48. *Ibid.* p. 2.

49. *Ibid.* p. 50.

50. Young, *Toadstool Millionaires,* p. 160, 205-12. Much of the early criticism, however, focused on preparations marketed to the physician rather than to the public.

51. Rush Medical College Matriculation Book, Rush-Presbyterian-St. Luke's Medical Center Archives. Miles' non-membership in the Elkhart County Medical Association from 1888 may be significant; however, there are no records of a censure. (Membership lists and minutes, kept by ECMA secretary).

52. *Modern Miracles,* p. 3.

53. Elkhart County Auditor, Commissioners' Papers, June 1893 and Dec. 1893 terms, Elkhart County Historical Society Archives. In the latter case, he wrote, "...no charge was made, as I regarded his case as practically incurable and gave him the medicine as a matter of charity." (Miles to George Milburn, Nov. 22, 1893, Commissioners' Papers, Dec. 1893.)

54. Much evidence shows that both Dr. Miles and the Beardsleys preferred that Dr. Miles not be involved in the regular operations of the company. One family account, however, claims that at some point Miles wanted the clinic to be incorporated into the medical company, but the company principals did not agree (Charles Foster Miles, Interview Notes 1975, Research Notebooks).

Chapter 5

1. *The Lakeside Annual Directory of the City of Chicago* (Chicago: Chicago Directory Co.), editions of 1894, 1896 and 1897 show Miles at three Hyde Park addresses; the 1895 directory lists the Ontario Hotel. Myers and Wade, *Chicago: Growth of a Metropolis* (Chicago: University of Chicago Press, 1969), p. 90, 172, 200, describes and pictures the Hyde Park neighborhood.

2. Miles' office in the Masonic Temple is listed in *The Lakeside Annual Directories*, 1893-99. It is interesting to note that an Erastus Miles, manufacturer of "Electric Belts," is listed in the 1893-95 directory at 207 State St., near Miles' later Chicago office. Erastus was the name of Miles' grandfather. The *Chicago Inter-Ocean*, Oct. 9, 1893, describes the Masonic Temple; a brief sketch of Miles appears in *Unrivalled Chicago* (Chicago: Rand McNally, 1896), p. 117.

3. The *Dr. Miles Medical and Ocular Institute for the Special Treatment of Serious and Complicated Chronic Nervous and Eye Diseases* (Elkhart: Review Printing Co., 1893).

4. Warner, *Therapeutic Perspective*, p. 235-70.

5. The *Dr. Miles Medical and Ocular Institute*, p. 5. The brochure was printed before the Institute was fully developed.

6. Beeman is listed in the *Lakeside Directories*, 1893-96; also in *History of Medicine and Surgery and Physicians and Surgeons of Chicago* (Chicago:Biographical Publishing Corp. 1922), p. 20. Miles advertised in the *Chicago Blue Book* (Chicago, 1896). A female optician is shown in a drawing on p. 26 of the Miles pamphlet. Bass recalls hearing that Elizabeth worked for Miles in Chicago (Memoirs, p. 11).

7. *The Dr. Miles Medical and Ocular Institute*, p. 3.

8. *Ibid.* p. 21; p. 28-29.

9. *Ibid.* p. 13. A letter to Dr. R. J. Cramp, from Prof. W. A. Puckner, June 15, 1915 (in Miles files, papers of the Bureau of Investigation, Archives of the American Medical Association, Chicago) reported that the "Special Treatment" contained "bromide in a relatively large amount," but "iodids were not found."

10. *Ibid.* p. 18, 35.

11. *A New Era Dawning in Medical Science* (Chicago: Miles Medical Association, 1895), p. 99.

12. Miles to Miles Medical Co., Mar. 17, 1894, with comments by Albert R. Beardsley, in Historical Documents #4, Miles Archives.

13. *Elkhart Review,* Jan. 11, 1894, Mar. 28; Dec. 26, 1895.

14. Dr. Miles Anti-Pain Pill and Dr. Franklin Miles Restorative Nerve Plaster were registered July 12, 1896 with the U.S. Patent Office (*Official Gazette of the U.S. Patent Office*, v. 76 [1896], p. 472). The listing notes that the use of both names dated back to July, 1893. The introduction of Anti-Pain Pills at the World's Columbian Exposition of 1893 is described in interview notes, Franklin B. Miles, Research Notebooks.

15. Dr. Miles Medical Co., Minutes, v. 1, p. 32, Dec. 17, 1897. Labeling was reviewed and approved by Miles.

16. A. R. Beardsley replied, "When you are here again we will endeavor to arrange the matter." (Inscribed on Miles letter, Mar. 17, 1894, Historical Documents #4, Miles Archives.)

17. Dr. Miles Medical Co., Minutes, v. 1, p. 25-26, Feb. 1, 1894, Jan. 21, 1895;

promissory notes in early financial records; payments listed from Apr. 28, 1894 to Sept. 16, 1895 in Cash Books 3 and 4, 1894-96, Journal 2, 1893-99 and Ledger 3, 1895-99.

18. Biographical sketch of Cyrus Roys in *National Cyclopaedia of American Biography*, v. XVII, p. 337-38: obituary in *New York Times*, May 20, 1915; article in *Elkhart Weekly Review*, Feb. 2, 1898. Also in their circle may have been former Elkhart drug-makers Herbert Bucklen and John Primley, according to a description of a Roys party in Elkhart (*Elkhart Review*, Dec. 31, 1902). Lord Chesterfield's advice on friendships of a gentleman in *Letters to His Son*, Dec. 19, 1749.

19. Marriage noted in *Elkhart Weekly Review*, July 25, 1895. Bass discusses her mother and her parents' marriage in Memoirs, p. 2-3, 4-6, 10-11, 13-14; Video-tape; Interview Notes, p. 8-10, 12-17, 19-20, and Questionnaire, p. 3, 5, Research Notebooks; and recorded interview, Fort Myers Historical Museum, Fort Myers.

20. According to Frances Miles' death record (Death Records, v. H-14, p. 61, Sept. 29, 1904, Elkhart County Health Dept., Elkhart) Frances was 8 years, 11 months, and 29 days old at her death, placing her birth date at Sept. 30, 1895. There is no record of Frances' birth in birth records of Cook County, Illinois or Elkhart County, Indiana. Miles' story of Frances' debility is told by Louise Bass, Memoirs, p. 3, and Interview Notes, p. 19, Research Notebooks.

21. *Success* (Chicago: Miles Medical Association, 1895), p. 4.

22. *New York Times*, Sept. 23, Sept. 30 and Oct. 1, 1895; *Chicago Inter-Ocean*, Sept. 21, Sept. 29, Oct. 1, Oct. 2, Oct. 7, Oct. 8, 1895. *Elkhart Review*, Oct. 3, 1895.

23. *Ibid.* Oct. 3, 1895.

24. *Ibid.* Dec. 12, 1895; *New York Times*, Dec. 7, 1895.

25. *Elkhart Review*, Aug. 26 and Aug. 29, 1896.

26. *Ibid.* Sept. 26 and Oct. 24, 1896.

27. *Ibid.* May 5, 1897; *Lakeside Annual Directory*, 1898, 1899.

28. According to the *Elkhart Review* (May 24, 1899), Miles' "office force," which would accompany him back to Chicago, included Ace W. Conner, Dr. J. W. Beeman, Miss Theresa Nye, Miss Sadie Hosterman, Nelson Nusbaum and Will Smith.

29. *Elkhart Review*, Oct. 23, 1897; Elkhart City Directory; *Elkhart Review*, Nov. 23, 1898. Presumably the Second Street home was the former Lighthall house, which Miles inherited. Miles responded to the toast at a Washington's Birthday banquet at the Century Club (*Elkhart Review*, Feb. 26, 1898).

30. Political activity, *Ibid.* June 25, 1898. Parties: May 7, 1898; Nov. 23, 1898.

31. *Ibid.* (Dec. 12, 1895), reported a planned trip to Florida from Washington; however, Minutes, v. 1, Dec. 28, 1895 show him back in Elkhart. A European trip is mentioned in Franklin B. Miles, Interview Notes, Bass, Interview Notes, p. 8, Research Notebooks; report of planned trip in *Elkhart Daily Review*, June 20, 1901.

32. *Elkhart Review*, May 24, 1899.

33. *Dr. Miles Neuropathic Cure for Diseases of the Heart, Lungs, Stomach, Liver, Kidneys, and Nerves* (Chicago: Franklin Miles Association, 1902), p. 7, 12.

34. *Ibid.* p. 9.

35. *Ibid.* p. 23.

36. *Ibid.* p. 25.

37. *The Lakeside Annual Directories,* 1900 and 1901, list Miles' address. Electa Miles' wedding is detailed in *Elkhart Review,* June 23, 1900. Marian's wedding year is listed in her biographical sketch (Citizens Historical Association, Indianapolis, 1948). Earlier, Miles had rushed to prevent Marian's supposed planned marriage to a young man in Warsaw, Indiana (*Elkhart Review,* Sept. 16, 1899). In Interview Notes, Elisabeth Miles Crow describes Miles as the sort of father who set extremely high standards for his children's choices of spouse.

38. Elkhart County Recorder, Index of Deeds, Book 103, p. 380, Sept. 17, 1900; *Lakeside Annual Directory,* 1901.

39. *Elkhart Review,* Mar. 12, 1902; Mar. 19, 1902. The small Chicago office was made to sound impressive in Miles' advertisements, such as one in the *Pacific Christian Advocate,* Nov. 19, 1902, which gave his address as "207 to 223 State St., Chicago." The Elkhart location was not mentioned.

40. *Elkhart Review,* July 9, July 23, 1904 and Nov. 26, 1904; *Tenth Annual Report of the Department of Factory Inspection of the State of Indiana* (Indianapolis, 1906), p. 53.

41. *Elkhart Review,* May 10, 1902, *Elkhart Daily Review,* June 16, 1902, *Elkhart Review,* June 16, July 23, 1902, Sept. 19, 1903.

42. *Golden Rules of Health...*(Elkhart: The Grand Dispensary, 1905), p. 10.

43. *Ibid.*, p. 22-23.

44. Miles' interest in recording weather data is confirmed by Louise Bass in recalling her father's weather equipment at his Florida farm (Bass, Questionnaire, p. 6, Research Notebooks; tape at Fort Myers Historical Museum).

45. *Elkhart Review,* July 2, 1902, *Elkhart Weekly Truth,* July 10, 1902; *Elkhart Review,* Oct. 22, 1902; *Ibid.*, Dec. 16, 1903, June 14, 1904, Feb. 11, 1905, May 13, 1905, June 23, 1906.

46. *Ibid.*Aug. 13, 1902.

47. Copies of the *Miles U.S. Weather Almanac and Handbook of Valuable Information* published by Dr. Miles Medical Co. are in the Miles Archives, along with records of printing and distribution. The 1902 edition is the first one mentioned in the *Elkhart Review,* Feb. 15, 1902; installation of new printing equipment is noted in *Ibid.*, Apr. 6 and July 6, 1901. The Miles Archives also has Miles Calendars, 1903-41.

48. *Miles U.S. Weather Almanac,* 1902, p. 18, 28; 22.

49. The last "Dr. Miles Medical Co." advertisement appeared in the *Elkhart Review,* June 21, 1904; the first to carry the name "Miles Medical Co." appeared

Aug. 27, 1904. "Do not address" is in *General Directions for the Use of Dr. Miles' Restorative Tonic* (Elkhart: Dr. Miles Medical Co., Mar. 1907), back page.

50. Documents detailing the Dr. Miles' Plan, including a Retail Agency Contract, are in the Miles Archives. The "refusal to sell" policy would be followed through the 1940s.

51. *One Year of the Dr. Miles Plan* (Elkhart: Dr. Miles Medical Co., 1904), p. 3; obituary, *Ohio Druggist,* 1929, Historical Items #4, Miles Archives.

52. *Elkhart Review,* May 24, 1902, Nov. 5, 1902, Jan. 24, 1903; Nov. 8, 1902. The house, now a funeral home, is briefly described by Elisabeth Miles Crow and Tom Gutermuth in Research Notebooks. Miles' plans must have been aided when the company doubled its dividends on Dec. 30, 1901 (Minutes, v. 1, p. 38).

53. *Elkhart Review,* Apr. 1, 1903.

54. *Ibid.,* Oct. 11, 1902; Dec. 31, 1902.

55. *Ibid.* Sept. 14, 1904; Oct. 18, 1902, Apr. 4 and July 4, 1903, May 25 and June 15, 1904; July 6, 1904; Mar. 2, 1904. Charles Franklin Miles was elected a director of the Dr. Miles Medical Co. Jan. 5, 1905 (Minutes, v. 1, p. 40).

56. *Ibid.* July 29, 1903; July 23, 1904; Sept. 9, 1905.

57. Bass, Memoirs, p. 3; *Elkhart Review,* Sept. 28, 1904; *Elkhart Daily Truth,* Sept. 30, 1904; Death Records, v. H-14, p. 61, Sept. 29, 1904, Elkhart County Health Dept.

58. *Elkhart Review,* Oct. 22, 1904.

59. *Ibid.* Nov. 18, 1905. Miles' grandsons reported that Miles' Adamsville farm was run for him by Rob Hill, till it was sold along with his Christiana Lake property to Francis Compton about 1917 (Franklin B. Miles, Memoirs, p. 4; Edward L. Miles, Memoirs, p. 4).

60. Miles' grandchildren, all born within a few years, were Frank Miles Cleveland; John Hyde Collins, Jr. and Cathryn Ellen Collins; and Franklin Beardsley, Charles Foster, Martha Elisabeth and Edward Lawrence Miles. (Bass grandchildren born much later.) An accident while driving his new White Steamer is described in the *Elkhart Review,* May 30, 1906.

61. Masonic membership: see Deahl, listed in Chapter 2, note 1. Fifteen Circle: *Elkhart Review,* Dec. 16, 1905, Apr. 21, 1906.

62. *Ibid.* Jan. 28, 1905 and Feb. 8, 1905.

Chapter 6

1. *Fort Myers Press,* Feb. 2, 1906; Karl H. Grismer, *The Story of Fort Myers* (Fort Myers Beach: Southwest Florida Historical Society, 1982), p. 78-167.

2. *Fort Myers Press,* Mar. 22, 1906.

3. Grismer, *Story of Fort Myers,* p. 181-82; 182-84. Closed Grantee Index to Deeds 1887-1922, p. 75, Lee County Recorder, Fort Myers; *Fort Myers News-Press,* Nov. 17, 1974.

4. Louise Bass, Memoirs, p. 14; *Fort Myers Press,* May 30, June 27, 1907.

5. *Fort Myers Tropical News,* Apr. 2, 1929; *Dr. Miles Premium Farm* (published by Miles c. 1921, copy in Research Notebooks.) *Elkhart Review,* Feb. 8, 1908; *Fort Myers Press,* May 27, 1909.

6. *Fort Myers Press,* May 23, May 30, Aug. 1, 1907; Grismer, *Story of Fort Myers,* p. 175-77.

7. *Fort Myers Press,* Nov. 19, 1908, Dec. 24, 1908 and Feb. 3, 1910. The history of the Shell House is described in Bass, Memoirs, p. 1 and Bass, Videotape; in Marian B. Godown, "The Haunted House," *Fort Myers News-Press,* Oct. 29, 1978 (reprinted in *Elkhart Truth,* May 16, 1981); in Betsy Zeiss, *The Other Side of the River* (Cape Coral, Florida: Historical Cape Coral, 1983), p. 20-21; and in Franklin B. Miles, Memoirs, p. 2. According to Franklin B. Miles, the original shell finish was coated over with stucco.

8. Bass, Memoirs, p. 2, 10.

9. *Ibid.* p. 1, 3. According to Bass, Questionnaire, p. 1, Research Notebooks, it was not an official adoption. There is no listing in Lee County's adoption records.

10. *Fort Myers Press,* Nov. 19, Nov. 26, 1908; Closed Grantee Index to Deeds, 1887-1922, p. 75-76, Lee County Recorder.

11. Obituary, *Fort Myers Tropical News,* Apr. 2, 1929. According to Louise Bass' recorded interview at the Fort Myers Historical Museum, Miles later advised his children, "Hang on to as much of the river property as you can, because someday it will make you wealthy beyond your wildest dreams."

12. *Fort Myers Press,* May 28, 1908.

13. Miles' Notes on Florida Farm, Miles Personal Papers.

14. The skeptical opinion of locals is noted in Grismer, *Story of Fort Myers,* p. 304; Bass, Memoirs, p. 3; Prudy Taylor Board, "Down on the Farm," *Fort Myers News-Press,* Mar. 4, 1984. Examples of climatic damage were a severe hurricane in Oct. 1910 and a flood in the summer of 1912. Neither seems to have seriously damaged the Iona region (*Fort Myers Press,* Oct. 20, Nov. 3, Dec. 22, 1910 and Sept. 12, 1912). Miles' dock in downtown Fort Myers was damaged by the 1910 hurricane, according to Allen H. Andrews, *A Yank Pioneer in Florida* (Jacksonville: Douglas Printing Co., 1950), p. 54. Bass remembers minnows swimming in the house during the 1912 flood (questionnaire, p. 1, Research Notebooks). Frequently encountered local insects were described in H. E. Stevens, "Bugs and How to Control Them," *Fort Myers Tropical News,* June 17, 1921.

15. Notes on Florida Farm, Miles Personal Papers; *Fort Myers Press,* May 27, 1909, Feb. 3 and Feb. 17, 1910. *Bristol* (Indiana) *Banner,* Mar. 4, 1910.

16. Grismer, *Story of Fort Myers,* p. 304-05; Bass, Memoirs, p. 3; Bass, Video-

tape; Bass, tape at Fort Myers Historical Museum.

17. Article from *Florida Planter,* quoted in *Dr. Miles Premium Farm;* Notes on Florida Farm, Miles Personal Papers.

18. Miles' technique of enrichment of the mineral-poor soil is described in *Dr. Miles Premium Farm.* See also *Fort Myers Daily Press,* Oct. 8, 1917, and *Fort Myers Evening Press* (obituary), Apr. 1, 1929. Quantities of compost produced described in Notes on Florida Farm, Miles Personal Papers.

19. *Fort Myers Press,* Feb. 3, 1910; irrigation system described also in Bass, Interview Notes, p. 4, Research Notebooks; *Dr. Miles Premium Farm.* Use of dry farming in winter and wet farming in summer and fall is described in Board, "Down on the Farm," *Fort Myers News-Press,* Mar. 4, 1984.

20. Bass, Memoirs, p. 4; Bass, videotape; Bass, tape at Fort Myers Historical Society; Zeiss, *Other Side of the River,* p. 24; *Dr. Miles Premium Farm.*

21. *Fort Myers Press,* Dec. 24, 1908, Feb. 3, 1910; Grismer, *Story of Fort Myers,* p. 192-93; Zeiss, *Other Side of the River,* p. 26. The straightening of the river also removed some of the most beautiful scenery. Franklin B. Miles remembered "The Munk," Miles' launch, about 25 feet long, with a cabin (Memoirs, p. 1).

22. *Fort Myers Press,* Feb. 17, 1910; Grismer, *Story of Fort Myers,* p. 207.

23. Bass, Memoirs, p. 5; Bass, Interview Notes, p. 1, 4, Research Notebooks.

24. Party described in *Fort Myers Press,* Feb. 25, 1909; club in *Fort Myers Press,* Mar. 4, 1909, Apr. 1, 1909. Prizes were to be awarded periodically for the largest fish caught. Miles also was a member of the Fort Myers Yacht and Country Club (Grismer, *Story of Fort Myers,* p. 185).

25. Items on parties appeared occasionally in the *Fort Myers Press.* On Edison, see Bass, Memoirs, p. 6-7; Bass, Interview Notes, p. 21, and Edward L. Miles, Memoirs, p. 1, Research Notebooks. Susan Miles Yeckel notes that Edison's friends' names were "written" in small stones in the Edisons' garden walk, and that her great-grandparents' names were included.

26. Grismer, *Story of Fort Myers,* p. 179-208; *Fort Myers Press,* Feb. 27 and Apr. 2, 1908.

27. No records survive in the Miles Archives that would indicate how large a role Miles played in these crises of the proprietary industry in general, and his company in particular. With Miles' legal knowledge and interest in the company's legal affairs, it is hard to believe that he remained aloof. An obituary notes: "He believed in the standardization of retail prices and bore the brunt of an expensive law suit to carry out this principle" (*Ohio Druggist,* 1929, in Research Notebooks). The case *Dr. Miles v John D. Park* was a classic case in antitrust law.

28. Dr. Miles Medical Co. Minutes, v. 2, p. 1-6, June 1, 1911; D. E. Pedigo & Co., Miles company stock ownership history in cornerstone material 1938, Miles Archives.

29. Slow, steady decline of the Dispensary work force is documented in *An-*

nual Reports of the Department of Factory Inspection of the State of Indiana, 1907, p. 45; 1908, p. 69; 1909, p. 69; 1910, p. 78; 1913, p. 79.

30. *Golden Rules for Recovering Health and Prolonging Life* (Elkhart: The Dr. Miles Grand Dispensary, c. 1911), p. 15-17.

31. A bank brochure entitled *The Citizens Trust Company of Elkhart, Indiana, The New Bank* was in the possession of the late Tom Gutermuth of Hartzler-Gutermuth-Inman Funeral Home in Elkhart (the former Miles home on West Franklin St.). Miles' colleagues were Dr. Frederick C. Eckelman and dentist Dr. Stephen M. Cummins.

32. A New England trip, in which the family visited the farm where Miles had spent his summers in his youth, is remembered by Franklin B. Miles (Memoirs, p. 5) and Elisabeth Miles Crow (Interview Notes, Research Notebooks). The genealogy by Lucretia Belle Hamlin is now owned by Susan Miles Yeckel of Dallas, Texas. About 1916 the Christiana Lake Tavern was sold, along with the Miles Adamsville farm, to Francis Compton, and was operated as a resort for a number of years (Franklin B. Miles, Memoirs, p. 4; Edward L. Miles, Memoirs, p. 4; *Elkhart Truth,* Aug. 5, 1981). The tavern has been torn down, but some cottages and outbuildings remain.

33. G. M. Trevelyan describes a way of life remarkably similar to Miles' in Florida in *English Social History* (New York: Longmans, 1978), p. 357.

34. Bass, Memoirs, p. 1, 4-5; Bass, Videotape; Bass, "Life on the Plantation," p. 1; Bass, Interview Notes, p. 4, Research Notebooks, Zeiss, *Other Side of the River,* p. 22-29; Godown and Board, articles previously mentioned. The 1910 Federal Census of Fort Myers includes in their households 96-year-old uncle, Lorin C. Miles (presumably Lorenzo, brother of Charles Julius Miles), and a cousin, Edwin, and his wife and three children. Life on the farm and countryside resembled that described in the novels of Marjorie Kinnan Rawlings.

35. Fire-fishing is described in Bass, "Life on the Plantation," p. 2; Bass, Interview Notes, p. 5, 23, Research Notebooks; Franklin B. Miles, Memoirs, p. 2-3. Bass describes her mother's Christmas parties in Memoirs, p. 4. Medical duties noted in Bass, Videotape. Use of boats in daily life is described in Bass, Memoirs, p. 6; Zeiss, *Other Side of the River,* p. 21-28; Bass, Videotape; audiotape at Fort Myers Historical Museum; Franklin B. Miles, Memoirs, p. 2-3, 6; *Fort Myers Press,* Feb. 22, 1912 and Grismer, *Story of Fort Myers,* p. 159-63.

36. Bass, Memoirs, p. 4-5, 10; Bass, "Life on the Plantation," p. 1; Bass, Interview Notes, p. 11, 15, 20, Research Notebooks, and Videotape; Zeiss, *Other Side of the River,* p. 22. About 1917 the Miles took in the children of Elizabeth's childhood friend, who had died; their name was Andrews (Bass, Memoirs, p. 5, and Interview Notes, p. 15, Research Notebooks).

37. Elizabeth's storytelling is recalled in Franklin B. Miles, Interview Notes, p. 2, and Elisabeth Miles Crow, Interview Notes, Research Notebooks. Miles' frequent lectures to his grandchildren are a vivid memory of Franklin B. Miles (Mem-

oirs, p. 7), Charles Foster Miles and Elisabeth Miles Crow, and Edward L. Miles (Interview Notes, Research Notebooks). The children frequently resisted the "message," though they had much affection for Miles.

38. A family custom of argument without rancor described in Bass Memoirs, p. 6; Franklin B. Miles, Interview Notes, 1980, p. 2; Research Notebooks. Miles' teaching of manners and physical fitness is remarked in Bass, Interview Notes, p. 1, 6, Research Notebooks, and Franklin B. Miles, Memoirs, p. 2. The latter source also describes the tutoring of the grandchildren.

39. Bass, Interview Notes, p. 6, Research Notebooks; Bass, Memoirs, p. 12-13, and tape at Fort Myers Historical Museum; Bass, Interview Notes, p. 7, Research Notebooks; Bass, Memoirs, p. 13; Bass, Videotape, and Memoirs, p. 12.

40. Bass, Memoirs, p. 12; Bass, Videotape. Miles' ideas on religion are referred to by Bass in Memoirs, p. 4; Videotape; and Questionnaire, p. 6, Research Notebooks.

41. Poker playing is described in Franklin B. Miles, Memoirs, p. 4; Charles Foster Miles, Interview Notes, 1975, Research Notebooks; Edward L. Miles, Memoirs, p. 3, also mention bridge and rummy, and Miles' insistence that they use real money. Miles' knowledge, library, reading habits: Bass, Memoirs, p. 3, Interview Notes, p. 2, 8, Research Notebooks.

42. Bass, Interview Notes, p. 8; p. 1-2, 4, Research Notebooks; tape at Fort Myers Historical Museum; Memoirs, p. 14.

43. Listing in Deed Book 45, p. 459-67, Lee County Recorder.

44. Elizabeth Benevolent Society: Bass, Interview Notes, p. 15, Research Notebooks, and Elizabeth Miles' obituary, Fort Myers News-Press, Oct. 3, 1941; J. M. Porter's activities in *Fort Myers Press,* Jan. 23, Aug. 7 and Oct. 16, 1913. Welcome for Mrs. Marshall: *Fort Myers Press,* Apr. 30, 1914; war work of Elizabeth and Electa Miles: *Fort Myers Daily Press,* Dec. 14, 1917, Oct. 19, 1918 and *Fort Myers News-Press,* Oct. 3, 1941; Rachel Miles' charities in Bass, Interview Notes, p. 24, Research Notebooks.

45. *Fort Myers Daily Press,* Oct. 25, 1917.

46. *Ibid.* Oct. 8, 1917; Bass, tape at Fort Myers Historical Museum; Bass, Videotape; Bass, Interview Notes, p. 5, Research Notebooks; Franklin B. Miles, Memoirs, p. 2. According to Bass, Miles marketed the syrup. Franklin B. Miles saw the unrefined sugar cane boiled down to heavy syrup in vats.

47. *Fort Myers Daily Press,* Oct. 8, Nov. 26, 1917; *Ibid.* Oct. 25, 1917; Bass, Questionnaire, p. 3, Research Notebooks.

48. The bonanza in green peppers is noted in the *Daily Press* Oct. 8 and Dec. 13, 1917, Jan. 18, 1918, Jan. 4 and Feb. 15, 1919. Citrus packing operations described in Grismer, *Story of Fort Myers,* p. 195; *Fort Myers Press,* Mar. 4, 1909, Nov. 17, 1910. Truckers' organization and operations described in *Fort Myers Daily Press,* Oct. 30 and Nov. 6, 1917, Jan. 18 and Dec. 20, 1918, Jan. 4, 1919, Nov. 12, 1920, Jan. 1, 1921.

49. A lengthy interview concerning Miles' avocado growing is in *Fort Myers Daily Press,* Jan. 6, 1919. Displayed products pictured and described in *Dr. Miles' Premium Farm; Fort Myers Tropical News,* Apr. 2, 1929. Those of Iona and Lee County generally are described in *Fort Myers Daily Press,* Oct. 26 and Nov. 20, 1917, Feb. 23 and Dec. 6, 1918. Miles' advice on royal palms: *Ibid.* Nov. 23, 1917. Some prizes won are listed in Notes on Florida Farm, Miles Personal Papers.

50. The Governor and his party shown with Miles in *Dr. Miles' Premium Farm;* visit, *Fort Myers Daily Press,* Nov. 20, 1917.

51. Quote from Miles to A. H. Beardsley, Nov. 7, 1924, A. H. Beardsley Papers, Ruthmere (copy in notebooks, Miles Archives.)

52. *Fort Myers Tropical News,* Apr. 1, May 3, May 10, May 13, May 17, May 27, June 3, June 14, Oct. 7, and Nov. 29, 1921; Jan. 17, 1922. *Franklin Miles et al. v Iona Drainage District et al,* Mar. 15, 1921, Civil Case #1898, Court Records, Lee County Clerk.

53. Truckers' classes are described as "a new idea in agricultural schools" in the article "Agricultural School Promoted by Dr. Miles," *Fort Myers Tropical News,* Oct. 18, 1921. The amount of land cleared is less obvious in *Dr. Miles' Premium Farm.* Bass remembers the Truckers' School in Memoirs, p. 3-4; Videotape; tape at Fort Myers Historical Museum; also in Godown article.

54. Quote from Miles letter to A. H. Beardsley, Feb. 16, 1923; also Miles to Beardsley, Dec. 2, 1922, both in A. H. Beardsley Papers, Ruthmere Museum Archives, Elkhart.

55. Bass, Memoirs, p. 6, 14; tape at Fort Myers Historical Museum; interview notes, p. 4, Research Notebooks.

56. Miles obituaries, see Chapter 2, Note 2.

57. A. H. Beardsley to Miles, Apr. 25, 1925 and June 1, 1925, and Miles to A. H. Beardsley, May 20, 1925, A. H. Beardsley Papers, Ruthmere Museum Archives.

58. The hurricane and its effect: Grismer, *Story of Fort Myers,* p. 23; *Fort Myers Tropical News,* Sept. 19-23, 1926.

59. Deaths of Marian's husband and son: biographical sketch of Marian Collins, Citizens Historical Association, 1948. The Shell House fire is described by Franklin B. Miles, Memoirs, p. 6-7; in Bass, Videotape; and tape at Fort Myers Historical Museum; Interview Notes, p. 11, Research Notebooks. The 1926 hurricane blew down the garage at Poinsettia Place, according to Franklin B. Miles (Memoirs, p. 6).

60. Dr. Miles Medical Co., Minutes, v. 3, p. 23-31, July 28, 1924, Dec. 31, 1925. Arthur J. Cramp, M.D. (ed.), *Nostrums and Quackery,* v. II (Chicago: American Medical Association, 1921), p. 147-48, 521-24; Franklin B. Miles, interview notes, Research Notebooks).

61. Last years: see Louise Miles Bass, Memoirs, p. 11, Interview notes, Research Notebooks. Obituaries: Chapter 2, Note 2.

62. Obituary, *Fort Myers News-Press,* Oct. 3, 1941.

List of Items Pertaining to Franklin L. Miles in the Miles Archives

Notebooks

1. Personal Papers of Dr. F. L. Miles, c. 1860-1929, copies donated by the Miles family, 1 vol. (looseleaf notebook)
Letters from Charles Julius Miles, 1863-64
Documents of school attendance, 1864-1875
Autograph book, c. 1864-75
Letter book/commonplace book, c. 1867-70
Elkhart Museum documents, 1880
Letters from P. T. Barnum, 1888
Misc. items, 1870s-1890s
Florida Farm notes and other Florida items
Misc. family items

2. Research Notebooks, compiled by Martha M. Pickrell 1981-85, 10 vols. Include clippings, notes, copies of documents, interview notes, correspondence, copies of Miles publications, etc.

3. Copies of A. H. Beardsley correspondence (originals in Ruthmere Museum Archives)

Numbered Series
(Institutional Holdings of Archives, catalogued)

#1 Dr. Miles Medical Co. Cash Books, Ledgers, etc.
#2 Dr. Miles Medical Co. Payroll Books.
#3 Dr. Miles Medical Co. Account Books, Sales Records; includes Dr. Miles Ledger, 1882-85 and first Cash Book, 1885-88.
#4 Dr. Miles Medical Co. Legal Documents and Historical Items
Corporation Minutes
Articles of Association, 1885
Early Stock Certificates
AMA Items
Patent, Trademark, Label Registrations
Miles Obituaries, 1929
Beardsley Obituaries
Almanac distribution figures
Dr. Miles Letter, 1894
Notes and Checks, 1894

#5 Dr. Miles Grand Dispensary Publications, Literature, Form Letters, AMA and other Investigatory Items
#6 Dr. Miles Medical Co. Oversize Publications (1890s etc.)
#7 Miles Production Records 1910-1951
#8 Books from Dr. Miles' Library
#16 Oral Histories
#23 Photographs
#45 Publications, c. 1889 - (magazines, almanacs, etc.)

Publications Authored in All or in Part by Franklin L. Miles, in the Miles Archives
*Xerox copy

1. Items published by the Dr. Miles Medical Company, Elkhart (Note: from 1893, or earlier, company publications combined the work of Miles and advertising copywriters.)

New and Startling Facts for Those Afflicted With Nervous Diseases: An Illustrated Treatise on Sick and Nervous headache, Nervousness, Convulsions, Apoplexy, Paralysis, Sleeplessness, Nervous Prostration, Sexual Weakness, Epilepsy, Dyspepsia, etc. (c. 1889-91) 36 p.

The Family Physician: An Illustrated Journal for the People, v. 10 (c. 1891-92), 4 p.

Modern Miracles, v. 2, no. 3 (1893), 4 p.

The Doctor, An Illustrated Journal for the People, v. XI (1893), v. XI (1894) and v. XIII (1895), 4 p.

Dr. Miles' Medical Monthly, v. 1, no. 3 (1894-95), 4 p.

Famous Men and Women: Who Are They, no. 1 (1895), 4 p.

The Heart, the Human Engine (c. 1895-96), 8 p.

Short Talks With Dr. Franklin Miles LL.B. (c. 1896), 5 p.

The Sunshine of Good Health Is Better Than Gold or Silver: Dr. Miles' Restorative Remedies Restore Health (1896), 4 p.

Dr. Miles' Nervine Restored Our Health (1896), 8 p.

Dr. Miles' Nervine Restores Health (1897), 8 p.

Dr. Miles Prize Puzzle (1897), 4 p.

Dr. Miles' Hints on Health: A Review of the Triumphs of Science Over Disease (c. 1897), 4 p.

Dr. Miles' Nerve and Liver Pills for Constipation (c. 1898-99) 2 p.

Feel Your Pulse for About 5 Minutes (1899), 16 p.

Miles U.S. Weather Almanac and Handbook of Valuable Information (1902-42), 36 p. each

Know Your Heart (1904), 36 p.

The Nervous System: Its Influence Upon the Health of the Body (1904), 36 p.

General Directions for the Use of...(etc.) (directions packed with medications) (c. 1907-1920), 16-20 p.

Dr. Miles' Restorative Remedies and the Diseases for Which They Are Recommended (1914), 32 p.

Dr. Miles' Family Medical Guide (1914), 52 p.

2. Books and pamphlets published for advertising purposes by Miles and by his medical clinic (under the names Miles Medical Association, Grand Dispensary, etc.) (Here, too, copywriters' work supplemented Miles' at least from 1893.)

A Popular Treatise on Diseases of the Ear; Deafness, its Causes and its Cure (Elkhart: Mennonite Publishing Co., 1876), 36 p.*

Human Rights, A Quarterly Journal for the People, Devoted to the Physical, Mental and Moral Improvement of the American Race, v. 1, no. 1 (Elkhart: Mennonite Publishing Co., 1888), 20 p.*

The Dr. Miles Medical and Ocular Institute for the Special Treatment of Serious and Complicated Nervous and Eye Diseases (Elkhart: Review Printing Co., 1893), 36 p.*

A New Era Dawning in Medical Science: A New and Rational Treatment for Diseases of the Brain, Nerves, Heart, Lungs, Liver, Stomach, Bowels and Kidneys: Debility, Nervous Prostration, etc. (Chicago: Era Publishing Co., Miles Medical Assn., 1895), 140 p.*

Success, Devoted to the Highest Interests of Common Life, v. 1, no. 1 (Chicago: Success Publishing Co., Miles Medical Assn., 1895), 24 p.*

Dr. Miles Neuropathic Cure for Diseases of the Heart, Lungs, Stomach, Liver, Kidneys, and Nerves (Chicago: Franklin Miles Assn., 1902), 28 p.

Golden Rules of Health Deduced from the Lives of Many Famous Men Who Have Attained Ripe Old Age; How to Live One Hundred Years (Elkhart: The Grand Dispensary, 1905), 28 p.

Marvelous Results of Rest Cure When Applied to the Eyes and Nervous System by the Miles Method (Elkhart: The Grand Dispensary, 1906), 28 p.

Personal to Correspondents: Important Questions Answered (Elkhart: The Dr. Miles Grand Dispensary), 12 p.

Golden Rules for Recovering Health and Prolonging Life (Elkhart: The Dr. Miles Grand Dispensary, 1911), 28 p.

Startling Reports of Cures: 300,000 Patients Treated at Home (Elkhart: The Dr. Miles Grand Dispensary, 1919) 8 p.

$2.50—Sent Free—$3.75 (Elkhart: The Dr. Miles Grand Dispensary, 1919), 36 p.

Many So-Called "Incurable" Diseases Reported Soon Cured by an Improved Method (Elkhart: The Dr. Miles Grand Dispensary, 1919), 36 p.

Dr. Miles Premium Farm (Fort Myers, Florida: Franklin Miles Assn., c. 1921),

2 p.

3. Articles and miscellaneous short writings

"Causes of Grecian Greatness," (*Phrenological Journal,* 1870), reprinted in *Human Rights,* see above

"Marriage," *Elkhart Democratic Union,* Aug. 9, 1872

"Parental Empiricism," *Ibid.* Aug. 23, 1872

"Scientific Propagation of Man," *Ibid.* Sept. 6, 1872

"Stirpiculture," *Elkhart Observer,* Nov. 6, 1872*

"The Davenport Brothers," *Ibid.* Dec. 18, 1872*

"Children's Rights vs. Parental Empiricism," (*Chicago Tribune,* Aug. 12, 1874), reprinted in *Human Rights,* see above

"Facts Worth Remembering," *Elkhart Review,* Oct. 24, 1878*

Letters to editor, *Ibid.* May 7-13, 1881*

"Ocular Irritation a Cause of Nasal Afflictions," *Weekly Medical Review of St. Louis,* 1884, p. 111-12

Articles on Iona Drainage District, *Fort Myers Tropical News,* Apr. 1, May 17, June 14, 1921*

Index